Coaching Skills for Sales Managers

Making the Great Stride from ***Manager to an Effective Coach***

Gerard Assey

Coaching Skills for Sales Managers

Making the Great Stride from Manager to an Effective Coach

By

Gerard Assey

Published by:

Gerard Assey

19/18, Palli Arasan Street

Anna Nagar East

Chennai - 600 102

ISBN: 978-93-92492-23-5

(Image courtesy: Bruno Nascimento on https://www.Unsplash.com-Thank You)

Table of Contents

- ✓ Step by Step Process for 'Coaching Sales Techniques and Strategies'
- ✓ Coaching Questions that a Sales Manager can use on a Sales Coaching Session
- ✓ Role-Playing Scenarios
- ✓ Example of a Coaching Plan and Schedule
- ✓ Sample Format to Monitor and Evaluate Coaching Sessions
- ✓ Managing Remote Sales Teams: Strategies and Best Practices for Coaching Success
- ✓ Handling Sales Personnel Attitude and Habits for Improved Performance
- ✓ Motivating and Inspiring Sales Teams
- ✓ Overcoming Challenges in Sales Coaching
- ✓ Handling Coaching Resistance from Sales Personnel
- ✓ Dealing with Difficult Conversations
- ✓ Handling Underperforming Salespeople
- ✓ Coaching for Growth and Career Development
- ✓ Coaching for Sales Team Collaboration
- ✓ Measuring Coaching Effectiveness
- ✓ Gauging the Effectiveness of Coaching Through Various Indicators and Key Performance Metrics
- ✓ Coaching for Sales Managers

Introduction

Welcome to **'Coaching Skills for Sales Managers -** *Making the Great Stride from Manager to an Effective Coach.'*

In today's dynamic business landscape, the role of sales managers has evolved beyond traditional managerial functions. The success of a sales team is no longer solely dependent on the manager's ability to direct and control; it now hinges on their skill to coach and develop their team members.

The transition from a manager to a coach is a powerful shift that can revolutionize the way sales teams operate and achieve their goals. Coaching empowers individuals, unlocks their potential, and fosters a culture of continuous learning and growth. By adopting a coaching approach, sales managers can inspire their team members to reach new levels of success, enhance performance, and drive exceptional results.

This book is designed to equip sales managers with the knowledge, tools, and strategies they need to make this leap from manager to coach. Whether you are a seasoned sales manager looking to enhance your coaching skills or a newly appointed manager seeking guidance on how to effectively develop your team, this book will serve as your comprehensive resource.

In this book, we will explore various aspects of coaching skills for sales managers, providing you with practical insights, actionable techniques, and real-life examples. You will learn how to build strong relationships, set clear expectations, assess performance, develop sales skills, motivate and inspire your team, overcome coaching challenges, and lead with a coaching mindset.

Each chapter is carefully crafted to provide you with a deep understanding of the key concepts and principles of coaching, along with specific examples and strategies tailored to the sales environment. Additionally, you will find practical exercises, self-reflection questions, and coaching scenarios that will enhance your learning experience and help you apply the concepts in real-world situations.

By the end of this book, you will have a solid foundation in coaching skills and the confidence to guide and develop your sales team effectively. You will be equipped with the tools to create a culture of growth, collaboration, and excellence, ultimately driving the success of both your team and your organization.

It's time to embark on this transformative journey from being a manager to becoming a coach. Are you ready to make the great leap?

Let's begin and unlock the full potential of your sales team!

The Role of Sales Managers, The Need for Coaching and Benefits

The Role of Sales Managers

Sales managers play a critical role in the success of any sales organization. They are responsible for guiding and leading a team of salespeople, setting sales targets, and ensuring that the team achieves its goals. Traditionally, sales managers have focused on managing their teams through tasks such as assigning territories, monitoring sales activities, and evaluating performance. However, in today's competitive business landscape, simply managing sales teams is no longer sufficient.

The Need for Coaching Skills

As sales environments become more complex and customer expectations evolve, sales managers must adapt their approach to effectively lead their teams. This is where coaching skills come into play. Coaching is a powerful tool that enables sales managers to go beyond traditional management techniques and truly develop their salespeople's potential.

Coaching in a sales context involves guiding, supporting, and empowering sales professionals to maximize their performance and achieve their full potential. It shifts the focus from solely managing activities and results to building individual capabilities and fostering a culture of continuous improvement. By adopting a coaching mindset, sales managers can inspire and motivate their teams to consistently excel, resulting in increased sales effectiveness and sustainable growth.

Benefits of Coaching in Sales Management

The adoption of coaching skills by sales managers offers numerous benefits for both individuals and the overall sales organization. Some key advantages include:

- ✓ Improved Performance: Coaching helps sales professionals enhance their skills, overcome challenges, and reach higher levels of performance. By providing personalized guidance and feedback, sales managers can help their team members identify their strengths and areas for improvement, ultimately leading to improved sales outcomes.
- ✓ Increased Engagement: Coaching creates an environment where salespeople feel valued, supported, and motivated. It fosters a sense of ownership, accountability, and self-confidence, leading to higher levels of engagement and job satisfaction.
- ✓ Enhanced Collaboration: A coaching approach encourages collaboration and teamwork within the sales organization. Sales managers who coach their teams create opportunities for knowledge sharing, peer support, and collective problem-solving, fostering a culture of collaboration and continuous learning.
- ✓ Retention and Development of Top Talent: Sales professionals who receive regular coaching and development opportunities are more likely to stay with an organization and contribute to its long-term success. Coaching helps identify high-potential individuals,

nurture their skills, and create growth opportunities, reducing turnover and ensuring a pipeline of top talent.

- ✓ Adaptive Sales Skills: In today's rapidly changing business landscape, salespeople need to adapt their approach to meet evolving customer demands. Coaching equips sales professionals with the skills and mindset necessary to navigate shifting market dynamics, identify customer needs, and provide tailored solutions.

As a sales manager, acquiring coaching skills is essential to drive individual and team performance, develop a resilient and adaptable sales force, and achieve sustainable success in a competitive marketplace.

In the following chapters, we will explore the fundamental principles, techniques, and strategies that will empower you to make the great leap from manager to coach. We will delve into the art of building relationships, setting clear expectations, assessing performance, and developing sales skills. We will also address common challenges faced by sales managers and provide guidance on motivating and inspiring sales teams, fostering collaboration, and measuring coaching effectiveness. Together, we will embark on a transformative journey that will elevate your sales management approach and unlock the full potential of your team.

So, let's begin this exciting adventure and explore the world of coaching skills for sales managers.

Understanding Coaching

We will commence with the fundamental concepts of coaching and explore how it differs from traditional managing. We will also discuss the coaching mindset and its significance in the role of a sales manager.

Defining Coaching

Coaching is a collaborative and transformative process that aims to facilitate an individual's growth, development, and achievement of specific goals. It involves guiding and supporting individuals through thoughtful questioning, active listening, and constructive feedback to enhance their skills, knowledge, and performance.

Coaching focuses on empowering individuals to discover their own solutions and take ownership of their development. Unlike traditional managing, which often involves directing and telling, coaching emphasizes facilitating personal growth, self-awareness, and self-reflection.

Coaching vs. Managing

While coaching and managing share some similarities, it is important to distinguish between the two. Managing typically involves overseeing tasks, assigning responsibilities, and ensuring that work is completed to meet predetermined objectives. It is more directive and task-oriented in nature.

Coaching, on the other hand, takes a more collaborative and developmental approach. It focuses on empowering individuals to tap into ***their*** potential, fostering a growth mindset, and facilitating their personal and professional growth. Coaching encourages individuals to think critically, explore different perspectives, and take ownership of their actions and outcomes.

The Coaching Mindset

Adopting a coaching mindset is crucial for sales managers who want to transition from being mere managers to effective coaches. The coaching mindset involves several key elements:

- ✓ Curiosity: Coaches are naturally curious and seek to understand the unique perspectives, challenges, and aspirations of their team members. They ask open-ended questions, actively listen, and show genuine interest in the individual's growth journey.
- ✓ Empathy: Coaches empathize with their team members, recognizing that each person has their own experiences, strengths, and areas for improvement. They create a safe and supportive environment where individuals feel understood, valued, and encouraged.
- ✓ Growth Orientation: Coaches believe in the potential for growth and development in every individual. They focus on building upon strengths, addressing weaknesses, and nurturing a growth mindset that encourages continuous learning and improvement.
- ✓ Trust and Respect: Coaches build trust and mutual respect with their team members. They create a foundation of trust by maintaining confidentiality, demonstrating integrity, and honoring commitments. They respect the individual's autonomy, opinions, and perspectives.

- ✓ Active Listening: Coaches practice active listening, a skill that involves fully engaging with the speaker, understanding their message, and validating their feelings and concerns. They refrain from interrupting, judging, or imposing their own agenda, allowing the individual to express themselves openly.
- ✓ Feedback and Support: Coaches provide constructive feedback and support to help individuals grow and achieve their goals. They offer specific and actionable suggestions, celebrate successes, and provide guidance during challenging times.

By cultivating a coaching mindset, sales managers can create a positive and empowering environment that nurtures their team members' potential and drives exceptional performance.

Understanding the distinction between coaching and managing and embracing the coaching mindset are crucial steps for sales managers on their journey to becoming effective coaches. In the next chapter, we will explore the importance of building relationships as a foundation for successful coaching interactions.

Understanding the ROI Gained by Implementing an Effective Sales Coaching

Implementing effective sales coaching in organizations can yield a significant return on investment (ROI) by improving sales performance, increasing revenue, and fostering professional growth and development.

Here are several key ROI benefits that can be achieved through the implementation of sales coaching:

Increased Sales Revenue:

- ✓ Effective sales coaching can lead to improved sales performances, resulting in increased revenue generation for the organization.
- ✓ Sales coaching helps sales professionals refine their skills, enhance their sales techniques, and overcome obstacles, ultimately leading to better sales outcomes.
- ✓ Example: A company implements a structured sales coaching program and observes a 15% increase in the average deal size and a 20% increase in the conversion rate of leads, resulting in a substantial boost in overall sales revenue.

Improved Sales Performance:

- ✓ Sales coaching helps salespeople enhance their skills, knowledge, and sales techniques, leading to improved sales performance.
- ✓ Coached sales representatives can make more effective calls, close deals more

effectively, increase their average deal size, and achieve higher win rates.

- ✓ Example: Company A implemented a sales coaching program that focused on refining negotiation skills. As a result, the sales team's average deal size increased by 15%, resulting in a significant boost in revenue.

Increased Sales Productivity:

- ✓ Sales coaching helps salespeople prioritize tasks, improve time management, and adopt efficient sales processes.
- ✓ Coached sales representatives can maximize their productivity, leading to increased sales activities and more meaningful customer interactions.
- ✓ Example: Company B implemented a sales coaching initiative that provided time management techniques and sales productivity tools. As a result, the sales team's average number of daily customer interactions increased by 20%, resulting in a higher conversion rate and overall sales growth.

Improved Sales Performance Metrics:

- ✓ Effective sales coaching contributes to improved performance metrics, such as call rates, conversion rates, win rates, and average deal size.
- ✓ By identifying individual strengths and areas for improvement, coaching helps sales professionals refine their approaches, tailor their messaging, and increase their success rates at each stage of the sales process.
- ✓ Example: After implementing targeted coaching sessions focusing on objection handling and negotiation skills, a sales team

experiences a 25% increase in their win rate and a 20% decrease in the average sales cycle duration, resulting in improved overall sales performance metrics.

Reduced Employee Turnover- Employee Retention :

- ✓ Effective sales coaching creates a positive and supportive work environment, enhancing job satisfaction and reducing employee turnover.
- ✓ Coached sales representatives feel valued, supported, and engaged, leading to increased job commitment and retention.
- ✓ Example: Company C implemented a sales coaching program that focused on professional development and career growth. The sales team turnover rate decreased by 30%, resulting in cost savings associated with recruiting, on-boarding, and training new sales personnel.

Enhanced Customer Satisfaction and Loyalty:

- ✓ Sales coaching improves salespeople's ability to understand customer needs, provide tailored solutions, and deliver exceptional customer experiences.
- ✓ Coached sales representatives can build stronger relationships with customers, leading to higher customer satisfaction and loyalty.
- ✓ Example: Company D implemented a sales coaching initiative that emphasized active listening and effective questioning techniques. As a result, customer satisfaction scores increased by 25%, leading to increased customer retention and referrals.

Improved Sales Forecasting and Accuracy:

- ✓ Sales coaching enhances salespeople's ability to gather accurate customer information, assess buying signals, and make more precise sales forecasts.
- ✓ Coached sales representatives can provide more accurate sales projections, helping sales managers make informed decisions and allocate resources effectively.
- ✓ Example: Company E implemented a sales coaching program that focused on improving pipeline management and sales forecasting. As a result, the sales team's sales forecasting accuracy improved by 20%, leading to better resource allocation and revenue projections.

Knowledge Transfer and Succession Planning:

- ✓ Sales coaching facilitates knowledge transfer and ensures continuity within sales organizations.
- ✓ As experienced sales professionals coach and mentor junior team members, they pass on their expertise, best practices, and industry knowledge. This knowledge transfer strengthens the organization's talent pool and supports succession planning efforts.
- ✓ Example: Through a structured coaching program, senior sales representatives share their expertise and provide guidance to new hires, accelerating their learning curve and enabling them to contribute to the organization's success more quickly. This knowledge transfer also ensures a smooth transition when senior sales professionals retire or move into different roles.

Leadership Development:

- ✓ Sales coaching develops the leadership skills of sales managers, enabling them to effectively guide and inspire their teams.
- ✓ Coached sales managers can drive team performance, cultivate a culture of success, and develop future leaders within the organization.
- ✓ Example: Company F implemented a sales coaching initiative that provided leadership training for sales managers. As a result, the sales managers' ability to motivate and develop their teams improved, leading to higher team morale and overall sales growth.

These examples illustrate the significant ROI that organizations can achieve by implementing effective sales coaching programs. The combination of improved sales performance, increased sales productivity, reduced employee turnover, enhanced customer satisfaction, improved sales forecasting, and leadership development contributes to the overall success and profitability of sales organizations.

When to Use Sales Coaching and When Not To

Sales coaching is a valuable tool for developing and improving the skills and performance of sales teams. However, it's important to understand when to use sales coaching and when not to. Here's a detailed explanation with examples:

When to Use Sales Coaching:

- ✓ **Skill Development**: Use sales coaching when there's a need to develop or enhance specific skills. For example, if a salesperson needs to improve their negotiation skills, coaching can be employed to provide guidance, practice, and feedback.
- ✓ **Performance Improvement**: Sales coaching is beneficial when a team member is underperforming and needs support to meet their sales targets. The coaching process can help identify the root causes of poor performance and provide solutions to address them.
- ✓ **New Product or Service Launch**: When a new product or service is introduced, sales coaching can be used to ensure the sales team is well-prepared to effectively communicate its value to customers. This includes training on product knowledge, objection handling, and sales strategies related to the new offering.
- ✓ **On-boarding New Salespeople**: New sales team members require coaching to get up to speed with the company's products, sales

processes, and best practices. Sales coaching can expedite their integration into the team and help them become productive quickly.

- ✓ **Sales Strategy Alignment**: When there's a need to align the sales team with new strategies, coaching can help convey the changes, address questions, and guide salespeople on how to implement these strategies effectively.
- ✓ **Continuous Learning and Development**: Sales coaching is useful for maintaining a culture of continuous learning and development within the organization. Regular coaching sessions can keep sales teams engaged, motivated, and up-to-date with industry trends and best practices.

When NOT to Use Sales Coaching:

- ✓ **Personality Conflicts**: Sales coaching may not be suitable to resolve deep-seated personality conflicts or interpersonal issues within the team. In such cases, it's often better to involve HR or a mediator to address the root causes of the conflict.
- ✓ **Lack of Clear Objectives**: If there aren't clear objectives or goals for a coaching session, it may not be the right time to coach. Coaching should always have a well-defined purpose and expected outcomes.
- ✓ **Unwillingness to Improve**: When a salesperson consistently demonstrates a lack of willingness to improve, coaching may not be effective. In such cases, it's important for management to consider other options, such

as performance improvement plans or, in extreme cases, termination.

- ✓ **Emergency Situations**: Sales coaching is not the appropriate response in emergency or crisis situations. For example, if a salesperson makes a significant ethical violation or there's a product recall, immediate action may be needed, such as legal consultation or corrective actions, rather than coaching.
- ✓ **Highly Specialized Expertise**: In situations requiring highly specialized expertise, coaching might not be the most efficient solution. For instance, if a sales team needs detailed technical knowledge about a complex product, it may be more efficient to provide in-depth training or access to subject-matter experts.
- ✓ **Temporary Performance Dips**: Not every minor dip in performance warrants a coaching intervention. Sometimes, a salesperson may face a temporary setback, like personal issues, which can affect their performance. In such cases, offering support, understanding, and temporary adjustments may be more appropriate.

In summary, sales coaching is a powerful tool for improving sales team performance, but it's important to use it judiciously. It should be applied when clear goals and objectives can be defined, and there's a genuine opportunity for skill development and performance improvement. In situations where other factors like personality conflicts or unwillingness to improve are at play, alternative approaches may be more effective.

Why and How is Every Great Sales Manager Required to Be a Great Coach

Every great sales manager should also be a great coach because coaching is integral to driving a high-performing sales team. Here's why this is the case and how it can be achieved effectively:

Why Every Great Sales Manager Should Be a Great Coach:

- ✓ **Skill Development**: Effective coaching helps salespeople develop the skills and knowledge they need to excel in their roles. This includes mastering sales techniques, product knowledge, objection handling, and negotiation skills. A great sales manager recognizes that continuous skill development is critical for success and actively supports it.
- ✓ **Performance Improvement**: Sales coaching enables managers to identify areas where salespeople are underperforming and create targeted strategies to improve their performance. This can involve setting clear goals, providing regular feedback, and offering guidance on how to overcome obstacles.
- ✓ **Employee Engagement**: Coaching fosters a sense of engagement and ownership among sales team members. When they know their manager is invested in their growth and development, they're more likely to feel motivated and committed to their roles. This, in turn, boosts morale and job satisfaction.

- ✓ **Retention and Team Development**: A great sales manager understands the importance of retaining top talent. By coaching and developing salespeople, they not only enhance individual performance but also contribute to the long-term success of the team and the organization.
- ✓ **Effective Communication**: Sales coaching promotes open and effective communication within the team. It encourages salespeople to voice their concerns, share insights, and seek help when needed. When a manager serves as a coach, they create a culture of collaboration and dialogue.

How to Be a Great Sales Manager and Coach:

- ✓ **Lead by Example**: Great sales managers should model the behavior they want their sales team to exhibit. If a manager expects their team to be punctual, professional, and customer-focused, they should demonstrate these qualities consistently.
  Example: If punctuality is important, the manager should always arrive on time for meetings and encourage the same behavior from their team.
- ✓ **Set Clear Expectations**: Effective sales coaching begins with clear expectations. Sales managers should communicate performance targets, KPIs, and behavioral expectations. This clarity helps salespeople understand what is required for success.
  Example: A sales manager may set clear expectations for the number of cold calls each

salesperson should make daily and the conversion rates they should achieve.

- ✓ **Provide Ongoing Feedback**: Constructive feedback is a cornerstone of sales coaching. Managers should offer regular, specific, and actionable feedback to help salespeople understand their strengths and areas needing improvement.

  Example: During a one-on-one coaching session, a manager can provide feedback on a recent sales call, highlighting what went well and offering suggestions for improvement.
- ✓ **Individualize Coaching**: Recognize that each salesperson has unique strengths and weaknesses. Effective sales managers tailor their coaching to the individual needs of each team member.

  Example: For a salesperson struggling with objection handling, the manager may provide additional training and role-playing exercises focused on overcoming objections.
- ✓ **Motivate and Recognize**: Sales managers should motivate their team through recognition and incentives. Acknowledging achievements, whether big or small, can boost morale and drive better performance.

  Example: The manager may implement a monthly "Top Performer" recognition program that rewards the salesperson with the highest sales figures.
- ✓ **Provide Development Opportunities**: Great coaches also identify opportunities for skill development. This may involve offering access to training, workshops, or mentorship programs.

Example: The manager can recommend a negotiation skills workshop for a salesperson looking to improve in that area.

- ✓ **Create a Learning Culture**: Encourage a culture of continuous learning and improvement within the sales team. This includes promoting the sharing of best practices and lessons learned.

  Example: Implement regular knowledge-sharing sessions where salespeople can share successful sales strategies and learn from one another.

Every great sales manager must be a great coach because coaching is fundamental to developing, motivating, and retaining a high-performing sales team. It involves leading by example, setting clear expectations, providing ongoing feedback, individualizing coaching, motivating and recognizing achievements, offering development opportunities, and fostering a culture of continuous learning and improvement. When sales managers embody these coaching principles, they drive success not only for their sales team but also for the organization as a whole.

Why is it Important to Wear the Hat of a Sales Coach?

Wearing the hat of a sales coach rather than a sales manager is essential for several reasons:

1. **Empowerment and Ownership**: Sales coaching empowers salespeople to take ownership of their own development and performance. It encourages them to identify areas for improvement and actively work on them, fostering a sense of autonomy and accountability.
2. **Continuous Learning**: A sales coach promotes a culture of continuous learning. By emphasizing the role of a coach, you encourage salespeople to seek knowledge, refine their skills, and adapt to changing market dynamics and customer expectations.
3. **Individualized Guidance**: Sales coaching recognizes that every salesperson is unique, with distinct strengths and weaknesses. A coach tailors their guidance to the individual needs of each sales team member, offering personalized support.
4. **Positive Feedback Loop**: Coaching creates a positive feedback loop. When salespeople receive constructive feedback, they are more likely to act on it and see positive results. This, in turn, boosts their confidence and motivation.
5. **Skill Development**: Sales coaching focuses on skill development. It helps salespeople master sales techniques, handle objections effectively, and improve their product

knowledge and negotiation skills. This is essential for long-term success.

6. **Performance Improvement**: Coaching aims at improving performance, not just monitoring it. It identifies areas where salespeople are underperforming and provides strategies to address those weaknesses.
7. **Relationship Building**: Sales coaches often emphasize relationship-building skills. Developing strong relationships with customers, based on trust and understanding, is crucial for sustainable success in sales.
8. **Adaptation and Innovation**: A coaching approach encourages salespeople to be adaptable and innovative. It allows them to experiment with new approaches, refine their strategies, and explore creative solutions to challenges.
9. **Mentorship and Support**: A coach acts as a mentor and a source of support. They offer guidance, encouragement, and a listening ear. This support is crucial, especially during challenging times or when salespeople encounter obstacles.
10. **Enhanced Motivation**: Sales coaching can boost motivation by recognizing and celebrating achievements, no matter how small. This positive reinforcement reinforces the value of effort and continuous improvement.
11. **Effective Communication**: A coaching approach promotes effective communication. Salespeople feel more comfortable discussing their challenges, asking questions, and seeking guidance in a coaching relationship.

12. **Long-Term Success**: Sales coaching contributes to long-term success. It's not just about short-term results but about equipping salespeople with the skills and mindset needed to excel consistently over time.

By adopting the hat of a sales coach rather than just a sales manager, you create an environment where salespeople feel supported, motivated, and invested in their own growth and success. It's about more than just managing performance; it's about fostering an atmosphere of continuous improvement and personal development, which ultimately benefits the sales team and the organization as a whole.

Creating the Right Sales Coaching Environment

In the realm of sales coaching, the environment in which coaching takes place plays a vital role in the effectiveness of the process. A conducive coaching environment fosters open communication, trust, and collaboration between the coach and sales team members. This chapter will delve into the key elements and strategies to create the right sales coaching environment, ensuring optimal learning, growth, and success.

Establishing Psychological Safety:

- ✓ Encourage an environment where team members feel safe to express their thoughts, ideas, and concerns without fear of judgment or retribution.
- ✓ Foster a culture that values honesty, transparency, and constructive feedback.
- ✓ Create an atmosphere where mistakes are seen as learning opportunities rather than failures.

  Example: The sales manager openly shares personal experiences of failures and challenges to normalize the learning process and encourage team members to take risks and learn from their own experiences.

Building Trust and Rapport:

- ✓ Invest time in building relationships and developing trust with team members.
- ✓ Demonstrate integrity, reliability, and confidentiality in all interactions.

- ✓ Show genuine care for the well-being and professional development of each salesperson.
  Example: The coach holds regular one-on-one meetings to discuss personal and professional goals, listen to concerns, and offer support and guidance. This builds trust and rapport between the coach and sales team members.

Cultivating a Growth Mindset:

- ✓ Foster a culture that embraces continuous learning, improvement, and development.
- ✓ Encourage a growth mindset, where challenges and setbacks are viewed as opportunities for growth rather than obstacles.
- ✓ Celebrate achievements and efforts made towards improvement.
  Example: The sales team participates in regular training sessions, workshops, and seminars to enhance their skills and knowledge. The coach highlights and recognizes individual and team growth, emphasizing the importance of continuous learning.

Providing Resources and Support:

- ✓ Ensure access to the necessary tools, resources, and technologies that facilitate learning and development.
- ✓ Offer ongoing support through coaching, mentorship, and guidance.
- ✓ Create opportunities for skill-building and professional development.
  Example: The sales manager provides access to a comprehensive sales toolkit, including sales playbooks, industry insights, and training materials. The coach also connects sales

team members with experienced mentors who can offer guidance and support.

Encouraging Collaboration and Teamwork:

- ✓ Foster a collaborative environment where team members support and learn from one another.
- ✓ Promote a sense of belonging and team cohesion.
- ✓ Encourage knowledge sharing, best practices, and cross-team collaboration.

  Example: The sales manager organizes regular team-building activities, such as group brainstorming sessions, peer coaching sessions, or collaborative sales challenges, to foster collaboration and strengthen team dynamics.

Promoting Recognition and Appreciation:

- ✓ Recognize and appreciate the efforts, achievements, and contributions of sales team members.
- ✓ Provide regular feedback and positive reinforcement for a job well done.
- ✓ Celebrate individual and team successes to boost morale and motivation.

  Example: The coach acknowledges and publicly recognizes outstanding sales performance during team meetings or company-wide announcements. This recognition reinforces a culture of appreciation and motivates other team members to strive for excellence.

Creating the right sales coaching environment is essential for fostering a culture of growth, collaboration, and continuous improvement. By establishing psychological safety, building trust, promoting a growth mindset, providing resources and support, encouraging collaboration, and recognizing achievements, sales managers can create an environment that enhances the effectiveness of sales coaching and drives the success of the entire sales team. The right coaching environment empowers sales team members to reach their full potential, exceed their targets, and contribute to the overall success of the organization.

Key Skill-Sets for a Good Sales Coach

Being a good sales coach requires a unique combination of skills and qualities that enable effective guidance and development of sales team members. Let's explore the key skill sets in detail, along with examples that illustrate their significance in the coaching process:

- ✓ Active Listening: A good sales coach possesses exceptional listening skills, allowing them to truly understand the needs, concerns, and aspirations of their team members. They actively engage in conversations, ask probing questions, and provide undivided attention to create an environment of trust and openness. For example, when a salesperson expresses frustration with a particular sales technique, the coach listens attentively, empathizes, and explores possible solutions collaboratively.
- ✓ Effective Communication: Strong communication skills are crucial for a sales coach to convey information clearly, provide feedback, and deliver constructive criticism. A coach must be able to articulate expectations, explain sales strategies, and communicate the importance of continuous improvement. Additionally, they should adapt their communication style to the individual needs and preferences of each team member. For instance, a coach might use visuals and real-life examples to illustrate a new sales technique during a training session.

- ✓ Empathy and Emotional Intelligence: A good sales coach demonstrates empathy and emotional intelligence by understanding and considering the emotions and perspectives of their team members. They create a supportive and inclusive environment where individuals feel valued, understood, and motivated. For example, a coach recognizes the challenges faced by a salesperson and provides emotional support while offering constructive feedback to help them overcome obstacles.
- ✓ Analytical and Problem-Solving Skills: Sales coaches need to be analytical thinkers who can assess performance metrics, identify skill gaps, and diagnose sales challenges. They use data-driven insights to provide targeted coaching and develop effective strategies. For instance, a coach might analyze sales data to identify patterns and trends, enabling them to design tailored training programs to address specific areas of improvement.
- ✓ Adaptability and Flexibility: A good sales coach is adaptable and flexible, capable of adjusting their coaching style to accommodate the diverse needs and learning preferences of their team members. They understand that each individual is unique and requires personalized coaching approaches. For example, a coach might modify their communication style, training methods, or goal-setting techniques based on the preferences and strengths of the salesperson they are coaching.
- ✓ Mentoring and Development: A sales coach serves as a mentor, guiding their team

members towards professional growth and development. They provide guidance, share knowledge and best practices, and foster a culture of continuous learning. A coach may conduct regular one-on-one coaching sessions, offer resources for self-study, or provide opportunities for skill-building workshops or training programs.

- ✓ Motivational Skills: A good sales coach knows how to motivate and inspire their team members to reach their full potential. They understand individual motivators, align goals with personal aspirations, and create a motivating environment that encourages high performance. For example, a coach may recognize and celebrate individual achievements, provide incentives and rewards for exceeding targets, or organize team-building activities to foster camaraderie and motivation.
- ✓ Time Management and Organization: Sales coaches must be skilled in managing their time effectively, as they juggle multiple responsibilities, including coaching sessions, performance evaluations, training programs, and administrative tasks. They prioritize tasks, set clear timelines, and ensure they allocate sufficient time for coaching activities.
- ✓ Continuous Learning: A good sales coach never stops learning. They stay updated with the latest industry trends, sales techniques, and coaching methodologies. They invest in their own professional development through attending workshops, reading books and

articles, participating in webinars, and seeking mentorship opportunities.

- ✓ Trustworthiness and Integrity: Sales coaches must build trust and maintain high levels of integrity with their team members. They act as role models, demonstrating ethical behavior and transparency. This fosters a culture of trust and respect within the sales team, enabling open communication and a willingness to learn and grow.

These key skill sets collectively enable a sales coach to effectively guide, develop, and inspire their team members. By continuously honing these skills, a sales coach can drive the success of their team and contribute to the overall growth of the organization.

Understanding the Barriers to Coaching

Barriers to coaching can arise within the sales manager-salesperson relationship or within the broader organizational context. These barriers can hinder the effectiveness of coaching efforts and limit the growth and development of sales teams. Let's explore some common barriers to coaching in detail, along with specific examples:

- ✓ Lack of Time: Sales managers often face time constraints due to numerous responsibilities and demands. This can result in limited availability for coaching, leading to rushed or infrequent coaching sessions.
  Example: A sales manager may struggle to find dedicated time for coaching due to their own workload, frequent meetings, or administrative tasks. As a result, coaching sessions may be sporadic or shorter than necessary.
- ✓ Resistance to Change: Some salespeople may resist coaching due to a fear of stepping out of their comfort zones or a belief that their existing methods are effective. They may be reluctant to adopt new strategies or make changes to their sales approach.
  Example: A salesperson who has been following the same sales techniques for years might resist coaching, believing that their tried-and-true methods are sufficient. They may resist suggestions for improvement or be unwilling to embrace new sales strategies.

- ✓ Lack of Trust and Relationship Building: Building trust between sales managers and salespeople is crucial for effective coaching. If trust is lacking, salespeople may be hesitant to open up, seek guidance, or accept feedback.

  Example: Salespeople who have experienced inconsistent or negative interactions with their sales manager in the past may struggle to trust their manager's intentions in coaching sessions. They may be less receptive to feedback or hesitant to share challenges or weaknesses.
- ✓ Organizational Culture and Support: The overall organizational culture and support can impact coaching effectiveness. If coaching is not valued or supported at the organizational level, sales managers may face challenges in dedicating resources or receiving recognition for their coaching efforts.

  Example: In an organization where the primary focus is on meeting short-term sales targets, coaching may be perceived as a secondary priority. Sales managers may face resistance in allocating time or resources for coaching, as the organization's culture prioritizes immediate results over long-term development.
- ✓ Lack of Training and Skills: Sales managers may face barriers to coaching if they themselves have not received adequate training or development in coaching skills. Without proper training, they may struggle to effectively deliver feedback, provide guidance, or employ coaching techniques.

Example: A sales manager who has recently transitioned from an individual contributor role to a managerial position may lack the necessary coaching skills and techniques. Without training, they may find it challenging to structure coaching conversations or provide constructive feedback.

✓ Inadequate Performance Metrics: If performance metrics and evaluation systems are not aligned with coaching objectives, it can undermine the effectiveness of coaching efforts. When salespeople are solely judged based on numbers without considering developmental goals, coaching may be perceived as less valuable.
Example: If salespeople are solely evaluated based on revenue generated and there is no consideration for skill development or long-term growth, they may prioritize short-term results over engaging in coaching conversations aimed at their overall improvement.

Overcoming these barriers requires a proactive and strategic approach. This can involve providing adequate time and resources for coaching, fostering trust and open communication, aligning coaching goals with organizational objectives, offering training and support for managers, and creating a culture that values and supports coaching as a critical component of sales team development.

Strategies to Create a Supportive and Open Environment that Promotes Effective Communication and Learning

Putting the sales representative or participant at ease before a coaching session is crucial for creating a supportive and open environment that promotes effective communication and learning. Here is an outline of strategies and examples to achieve this:

Establish Rapport:

- ✓ Greet the sales representative warmly and engage in small talk to build a personal connection.
- ✓ Use active listening and show genuine interest in their thoughts, experiences, and challenges.
- ✓ Example: *"Hi, John. How was your weekend? I heard you closed a significant deal last week. Congratulations! Tell me more about it."*

Create a Safe Space:

- ✓ Emphasize that the coaching session is a judgment-free zone where mistakes are opportunities for growth.
- ✓ Encourage open and honest communication by assuring confidentiality and non-punitive feedback.
- ✓ Example: *"During this coaching session, feel free to share your thoughts, concerns, and even areas where you feel you need improvement. This is a safe space for us to work together and grow."*

Clarify the Purpose and Benefits:

- ✓ Clearly communicate the objectives and benefits of the coaching session.
- ✓ Explain how the coaching will support their professional development and help them achieve their goals.
- ✓ Example: *"Today's coaching session will focus on refining your negotiation skills. By improving in this area, you will be able to secure better deals and enhance your overall sales performance."*

Set Expectations:

- ✓ Clearly outline the agenda, structure, and timeframe of the coaching session.
- ✓ Communicate what is expected from both the sales representative and the coach.
- ✓ Example: *"During the next 30 minutes, we'll review your recent sales calls, analyze your approach, and discuss areas of improvement. I encourage you to actively participate, ask questions, and provide insights from your perspective."*

Demonstrate Empathy and Support:

- ✓ Acknowledge the challenges and pressures faced by sales representatives.
- ✓ Show empathy and understanding, creating a supportive environment where they feel comfortable sharing their concerns.
- ✓ Example: *"I understand that sales can be demanding, and you face various challenges daily. I'm here to support you and provide guidance to help you overcome any obstacles you may encounter."*

Active Listening:

- ✓ Give the sales representative ample opportunity to express themselves and actively listen to their thoughts, ideas, and concerns.
- ✓ Demonstrate understanding and validate their experiences to foster trust and openness.
- ✓ Example: *"I want to hear your perspective on the recent client interaction. Please share what happened, how you handled it, and any challenges you faced. I'm here to listen and provide guidance."*

Use Positive Reinforcement:

- ✓ Start the coaching session by highlighting the sales representative's strengths, achievements, or recent successes.
- ✓ Reinforce their capabilities and build their confidence before addressing areas for improvement.
- ✓ Example: *"Before we dive into the coaching session, I want to recognize your exceptional performance in meeting last month's sales targets. Your dedication and hard work have not gone unnoticed."*

Encourage Questions and Input:

- ✓ Encourage the sales representative to ask questions, seek clarification, and actively participate in the coaching session.
- ✓ Create an open dialogue where their input and insights are valued.
- ✓ Example: *"Throughout the session, please feel free to interrupt or ask questions whenever you need clarification or want to delve deeper into a specific topic. Your input is*

essential to make this coaching session effective."

By implementing these strategies, sales coaches can create a comfortable and supportive environment for the sales representative before a coaching session. This establishes a solid foundation for effective coaching conversations, collaborative problem-solving, and continuous learning and growth.

Building Relationships

We will now further explore the importance of establishing trust, effective communication, and active listening, and provide specific examples to illustrate each concept.

Establishing Trust

Trust is the cornerstone of any successful coaching relationship. It creates an environment of safety, openness, and collaboration. Here are some strategies for establishing trust with your team members:

- ✓ Consistency and Reliability: Be consistent in your actions, decisions, and follow-through. If you promise to provide feedback by a certain date, ensure that you deliver on time. By consistently meeting your commitments, you demonstrate reliability and build trust.

  Example: As a sales manager, you consistently hold weekly team meetings at the same time and location. Your team members appreciate your consistency, as it shows that you value their time and prioritize regular communication.
- ✓ Transparency: Be open and transparent in your communication. Share relevant information about organizational changes, team performance, and goals. Keeping your team informed builds trust and fosters a sense of inclusion.

  Example: During a company-wide meeting, you openly discuss the challenges the organization is facing and the steps being taken to address them. By providing transparent communication, you demonstrate trustworthiness and credibility.

- ✓ Confidentiality: Respect the confidentiality of sensitive information shared by your team members. When individuals confide in you, ensure that their trust is honored by maintaining privacy. Confidentiality fosters trust and encourages open communication.
  Example: A team member expresses personal concerns regarding their performance. You assure them that their conversation will remain confidential, and you focus on finding solutions together without disclosing the details to others.

Effective Communication

Effective communication is vital for building relationships and fostering understanding. It involves clear, concise, and meaningful exchange of information. Consider the following communication strategies:

- ✓ Clarity: Clearly articulate expectations, objectives, and goals to avoid misunderstandings. Use simple and concise language to ensure that your messages are understood by all.
  Example: When assigning a new project, you provide clear instructions, outlining the scope, timeline, and desired outcomes. This clarity allows team members to understand what is expected and reduces confusion.
- ✓ Active Listening: Actively listen to your team members to demonstrate that you value their input and perspectives. Engage in the conversation, maintain eye contact, and ask

clarifying questions to deepen your understanding.

Example: During a team brainstorming session, you actively listen to each team member's ideas, nodding and paraphrasing to show your attentiveness. This active listening encourages open participation and builds rapport.

- ✓ Openness to Feedback: Create a safe space for team members to provide feedback. Encourage open and honest dialogue, actively seek input, and value different perspectives. Respond to feedback with respect and a willingness to address concerns.

  Example: After a client meeting, you ask your team members for feedback on the sales presentation. You express appreciation for their insights, acknowledging that their feedback is crucial for continuous improvement.

Active Listening

Active listening is a critical skill for effective coaching. It involves fully engaging with the speaker, understanding their message, and validating their feelings and concerns. Here are strategies for enhancing active listening skills:

- ✓ Be Present: Give your full attention to the speaker, eliminating distractions and showing genuine interest in what they have to say. Maintain eye contact and use body language to demonstrate engagement.

  Example: During a one-on-one coaching session, you put away your phone, face the team member directly, and actively listen to their challenges and aspirations. Your attentive presence creates a safe and supportive environment for open dialogue.

- ✓ Reflective Responses: Provide reflective responses to show that you have understood the speaker's message. Summarize their key points, paraphrase their statements, and ask clarifying questions to ensure alignment.

  Example: When a team member expresses frustration with a client, you summarize their concerns by saying, "So, if I understand correctly, you feel that the client's changing expectations have been causing difficulties in delivering the desired results. Is that correct?" This reflection demonstrates your understanding and encourages further discussion.
- ✓ Empathy and Validation: Show empathy and validate the speaker's feelings and concerns. Acknowledge their emotions and provide support without judgment. This fosters trust and creates a safe space for open communication.

  Example: A team member shares their anxieties about meeting aggressive sales targets. You respond empathetically, acknowledging the pressure they are under and offering reassurance by saying, "I understand that the targets can be challenging. I appreciate your hard work and dedication. Let's work together to identify strategies that can help you achieve your goals."

By actively building trust, practicing effective communication, and honing your active listening skills, you lay a strong foundation for meaningful and impactful coaching relationships with your team members. In the next chapter, we will explore the importance of setting clear expectations as a sales manager and coach.

Setting Clear Expectations

In this chapter, we will explore the critical aspects of setting clear expectations as a sales manager and coach. We will delve into the process of defining goals and objectives, utilizing SMART goals in sales coaching, and aligning individual goals with organizational goals. Through specific examples, we will illustrate each concept to provide practical insights.

Defining Goals and Objectives

Setting clear goals and objectives is essential for guiding the efforts of your sales team. Defining goals helps create a sense of purpose and direction, enabling individuals to focus their energy on meaningful outcomes. Consider the following strategies when defining goals and objectives:

- ✓ Specificity: Clearly articulate what needs to be accomplished. Vague goals can lead to confusion and lack of focus. For example, instead of setting a goal to "increase sales," specify a goal to "increase monthly sales revenue by 10%."

  Example: As a sales manager, you set a specific goal for your team to secure 20 new clients in the next quarter. This goal provides a clear target and aligns everyone's efforts towards achieving a specific outcome.
- ✓ Measurability: Establish specific metrics or key performance indicators (KPIs) to track progress and success. Measurable goals provide tangible evidence of achievement and enable you to assess performance.

Example: You set a goal for each sales representative to achieve a minimum of 50,000 in sales per month. This measurable target allows you to track individual performance and provide support to those who may need assistance.

- ✓ Attainability: Set goals that are challenging yet realistic. Consider the skills, resources, and support needed for individuals to achieve their goals. Goals should stretch their capabilities while remaining within reach.

  Example: One of your team members has consistently achieved 30,000 in sales per month. Instead of setting a goal of 100,000, which may be unrealistic, you set an attainable goal of 40,000 to encourage growth and maintain motivation.
- ✓ Relevance: Ensure that goals are relevant to the individual's role and aligned with their personal and professional aspirations. Connect the goals to the overall objectives of the sales team and the organization as a whole.

  Example: A sales representative expresses interest in developing their leadership skills. You set a goal for them to take on a mentoring role and provide guidance to a new team member. This goal aligns with their aspirations while contributing to the growth of the sales team.

Utilizing SMART Goals in Sales Coaching

SMART goals provide a structured framework for effective goal setting. SMART stands for Specific, Measurable, Achievable, Relevant, and Time-Bound.

Let's explore how each element applies to sales coaching through specific examples:

- ✓ Specific: Clearly define the desired outcome and actions required to achieve it. Specify what, why, and how the goal will be accomplished.
  Example: A sales representative's specific goal is to increase their average deal size by 15% within the next three months. This clarity allows them to focus their efforts on increasing the value of each sale.
- ✓ Measurable: Identify specific metrics or indicators that will be used to assess progress and success. Quantifiable measurements provide clarity and accountability.
  Example: A sales manager sets a measurable goal for their team to achieve a sales growth of 20% compared to the previous quarter. This metric enables them to track and evaluate performance accurately.
- ✓ Achievable: Set goals that challenge individuals to stretch their capabilities but remain within their reach. Goals should be ambitious yet realistic.
  Example: A sales representative has consistently achieved a monthly target of 50,000. Their SMART goal is to increase their monthly sales by 10% to 55,000. This goal pushes them to enhance their performance without overwhelming them.
- ✓ Relevant: Ensure that goals align with the individual's role, responsibilities, and the broader objectives of the sales team and organization. Goals should contribute to their growth and the overall success of the team.

Example: A sales manager sets a relevant goal for a team member to attend a sales training program focused on negotiation skills. This goal aligns with the individual's role and supports their professional development.

✓ Time-Bound: Set a specific timeline or deadline for goal achievement. A defined timeframe creates a sense of urgency and helps individuals prioritize their efforts.
Example: A sales team leader sets a time-bound goal for their team to close five new deals within the next two weeks. This deadline motivates the team to take immediate action and maintain focus on achieving the goal.

Aligning Individual Goals with Organizational Goals

Alignment between individual goals and organizational goals is crucial for driving collective success. When individual goals align with the broader objectives of the sales team and organization, it creates synergy and fosters a sense of shared purpose. Consider the following strategies for aligning individual goals:

✓ Cascading Goals: Start with the organization's strategic goals and then cascade them down to the sales team and individual goals. This ensures alignment at every level and helps individuals understand how their contributions support the larger objectives.
Example: The organization's strategic goal is to expand into a new market segment. As a sales manager, you cascade this goal to your team by setting a goal for each sales representative to acquire five new clients within the target market segment.

- ✓ Collaborative Goal Setting: Involve individuals in the goal-setting process to increase ownership and commitment. Seek their input, insights, and perspectives when defining goals.

  Example: During a team meeting, you facilitate a collaborative goal-setting session where team members contribute their ideas and suggestions. Together, you determine the most relevant and impactful goals for the team.
- ✓ Regular Communication: Continuously communicate the organizational goals and the rationale behind them. Share progress updates, milestones, and successes to keep individuals motivated and engaged.

  Example: As a sales manager, you conduct regular team meetings to discuss the progress towards organizational goals. You provide updates on key metrics, celebrate achievements, and address any challenges or adjustments required.

By setting clear expectations through defined goals and objectives, utilizing SMART goals, and aligning individual goals with organizational goals, you provide a clear roadmap for success. In the next chapter, we will explore the crucial role of providing constructive feedback and coaching for performance improvement.

Assessing Performance

We need to now get into the crucial process of assessing performance as a sales manager and coach. We will discuss the importance of performance metrics and key performance indicators (KPIs), various performance evaluation techniques, and the art of providing constructive feedback. Specific examples will be provided to illustrate each concept effectively.

Performance Metrics and Key Performance Indicators (KPIs)

Performance metrics and KPIs are essential tools for measuring and evaluating sales team performance. They provide tangible data and insights into individual and team achievements. Consider the following strategies when defining performance metrics and KPIs:

- ✓ Revenue Generation: Revenue is a fundamental metric that indicates the success of the sales team. It reflects the effectiveness of sales strategies and the ability to close deals.

  Example: A performance metric for a sales representative could be achieving a monthly sales target of 100,000.
- ✓ Conversion Rates: Conversion rates measure the percentage of leads or prospects that convert into customers. It reflects the efficiency of the sales process and the ability to persuade and close deals.

  Example: A KPI for a sales representative could be maintaining a conversion rate of at least 25% from leads to closed deals.

- ✓ Average Deal Size: Average deal size reflects the value of each sale made. It indicates the ability to upsell, cross-sell, and negotiate effectively.
  Example: A performance metric for a sales representative could be maintaining an average deal size of 10,000 or higher.
- ✓ Sales Cycle Length: The sales cycle length measures the time it takes to convert a lead into a closed deal. It reflects efficiency, effectiveness, and the ability to manage the sales process.
  Example: A KPI for a sales representative could be reducing the average sales cycle length from 60 days to 45 days.

Performance Evaluation Techniques

Various performance evaluation techniques can be utilized to assess sales team performance effectively. These techniques provide a comprehensive understanding of individual strengths, areas for improvement, and overall team dynamics. Consider the following performance evaluation techniques:

- ✓ Sales Metrics Analysis: Analyzing performance metrics and KPIs allows you to track progress, identify trends, and evaluate individual and team achievements. Regularly review the data to identify areas of success and areas that require attention.
  Example: By analyzing the monthly sales revenue and conversion rates, you can identify top-performing sales representatives and areas where additional coaching or support may be needed.
- ✓ Performance Reviews: Conduct regular performance reviews to discuss individual

performance, set goals, provide feedback, and address any challenges or concerns. These reviews provide a platform for open dialogue and goal alignment.

Example: During a performance review, you discuss a sales representative's achievements, areas for improvement, and collaboratively set goals for the upcoming quarter. This process allows for two-way communication and ensures clarity on expectations.

- ✓ Sales Role-Play Exercises: Role-playing exercises simulate real sales scenarios and allow you to assess individuals' sales skills, product knowledge, and ability to handle objections. It provides practical insights into their sales capabilities.

  Example: During a role-playing exercise, you simulate a sales call scenario, where a sales representative must engage with a prospective client and address common objections. Through this exercise, you can evaluate their communication skills, objection handling, and persuasive abilities.

Providing Constructive Feedback

Providing constructive feedback is an integral part of the performance assessment process. It allows you to address areas for improvement, celebrate successes, and guide individuals towards better performance. Consider the following strategies when providing constructive feedback:

- ✓ Timeliness: Provide feedback promptly, whether it is positive reinforcement or constructive criticism. Timely feedback allows

individuals to reflect on their performance and make necessary adjustments.
Example: After a sales presentation, you provide immediate feedback to a sales representative, highlighting their effective communication skills and suggesting areas for improvement in their delivery.

- ✓ Specificity: Be specific in your feedback, focusing on behaviors, actions, and outcomes. Specific feedback provides clarity and allows individuals to understand exactly what they need to improve.
  Example: Instead of saying, "You need to work on your presentation skills," provide specific feedback such as, "Your presentation lacked visual aids and concise messaging. Consider incorporating visuals and practicing your delivery to make a stronger impact."
- ✓ Balance: Strike a balance between positive feedback and constructive criticism. Recognize and celebrate achievements, but also provide guidance on areas that require improvement. Maintain a supportive and growth-oriented tone.
  Example: When providing feedback, acknowledge a sales representative's success in meeting their sales targets while also discussing opportunities for enhancing their negotiation skills to increase deal value.

By utilizing performance metrics and KPIs, employing performance evaluation techniques, and providing constructive feedback, you can assess performance effectively and guide individuals towards improvement. In the next chapter, we will explore the art of coaching for skill development and performance enhancement.

Coaching Techniques and Tools

As seen so far, coaching is an essential skill for sales managers to develop their team members and drive performance improvement. In this chapter, we will explore various coaching techniques and tools that can enhance the coaching experience. We will discuss different coaching approaches, coaching models and frameworks, and the effective utilization of technology in coaching. Specific examples will be provided to illustrate each concept effectively.

Different Coaching Approaches

Coaching is not a one-size-fits-all approach. Different situations and individuals may require different coaching techniques. Let's explore three common coaching approaches:

- ✓ Directive Coaching: In this approach, the coach takes a more authoritative role, providing clear instructions, guidance, and solutions to the coachee. This approach is useful when the coachee requires immediate direction or lacks experience in a specific area.

  Example: A sales representative is struggling with objection handling during client meetings. The coach adopts a directive coaching approach by providing specific objection handling techniques and role-playing scenarios to help the representative improve their skills.
- ✓ Non-Directive Coaching: Also known as "coaching from within," this approach focuses on helping the coachee discover their own solutions through self-reflection and

questioning. The coach acts as a facilitator, allowing the coachee to explore different perspectives and generate insights.

Example: A sales representative is facing challenges in closing deals. The coach adopts a non-directive coaching approach by asking probing questions to help the representative identify their strengths, uncover any underlying obstacles, and generate potential solutions.

- ✓ Collaborative Coaching: This approach emphasizes collaboration and joint problem-solving between the coach and coachee. Both parties work together to identify solutions, set goals, and develop action plans.

  Example: A sales manager and a representative collaborate to develop a sales strategy for a new product launch. They engage in joint brainstorming sessions, share ideas, and collectively create an actionable plan that aligns with the organization's goals.

Coaching Models and Frameworks

Coaching models and frameworks provide a structured approach to coaching conversations, ensuring that important aspects are covered. Here are two commonly used coaching models:

- ✓ GROW Model: The GROW model is a popular coaching framework that stands for Goal, Reality, Options, and Way Forward. It provides a systematic approach to help coachees clarify their goals, assess the current reality, explore options, and determine actionable steps.

  Example: During a coaching session, the coach employs the GROW model to guide the coachee in setting specific sales goals (Goal), assessing the current market conditions and their own performance (Reality), exploring different sales strategies and techniques (Options), and defining a plan of action with specific milestones and deadlines (Way Forward).

- ✓ OSKAR Model: The OSKAR model focuses on solution-oriented coaching and stands for Outcome, Scaling, Know-how, Affirm and Action, and Review. It helps coachees identify desired outcomes, assess their current strengths, generate ideas, commit to actions, and review progress.

  Example: The coach applies the OSKAR model by assisting the coachee in defining their desired outcome (Outcome), scaling their confidence on a scale from 1 to 10 (Scaling), exploring their existing sales knowledge and skills (Know-how), affirming their capabilities and identifying potential actions (Affirm and Action), and scheduling a review session to evaluate progress and make adjustments (Review).

Detailed Examples for the GROW and OSKAR Models:

The GROW Model:

The GROW model is a widely used coaching framework that provides a systematic approach to coaching conversations. It consists of four key steps:

- ✓ Goal: In this step, the coach helps the coachee clarify their goals and define what they want to achieve. The coach encourages the coachee to set specific, measurable, achievable, relevant, and time-bound (SMART) goals.

Example: During a coaching session, a sales manager works with a sales representative to set a goal of increasing monthly sales by 20% within the next quarter. The goal is specific, measurable, achievable, relevant, and time-bound.

- ✓ Reality: In this step, the coach assists the coachee in assessing the current reality or situation. This involves examining the coachee's strengths, weaknesses, resources, and any obstacles or challenges they may be facing.

  Example: The coach asks the sales representative to evaluate their current sales performance, identify their strengths in building customer relationships, and recognize areas for improvement, such as handling objections or closing deals.
- ✓ Options: In this step, the coach helps the coachee explore various options and alternatives for achieving their goals. The coach encourages brainstorming, creative thinking, and considering different strategies or approaches.

  Example: The coach engages the sales representative in a discussion to generate potential options for increasing sales, such as targeting new markets, improving product knowledge, enhancing networking efforts, or implementing a referral program.
- ✓ Way Forward: In this final step, the coach supports the coachee in determining a specific plan of action with clear steps, milestones,

and deadlines. The coach also ensures accountability and monitors progress.
Example: The coach and sales representative work together to develop an action plan, including activities such as attending sales training workshops, conducting customer satisfaction surveys, setting weekly sales targets, and scheduling regular check-ins to review progress.

The OSKAR Model:

The OSKAR model is a solution-oriented coaching model that focuses on positive outcomes. It stands for Outcome, Scaling, Know-how, Affirm and Action, and Review. Here's a breakdown of each step:

- ✓ Outcome: In this step, the coach helps the coachee identify and define the desired outcome or goal they want to achieve. The emphasis is on a positive and specific outcome.
  Example: The coach works with a sales representative to define a desired outcome of securing three new major accounts within the next quarter.
- ✓ Scaling: In this step, the coach asks the coachee to rate their current confidence or capability related to the desired outcome on a scale from 1 to 10. This helps the coachee assess their starting point and measure progress.
- ✓ Example: The coach asks the sales representative to rate their current confidence in acquiring major accounts on a scale from 1 to 10. If the representative rates their confidence as a 6, the coach can then work

with them to bridge the gap to reach a higher level of confidence.

- ✓ Know-how: In this step, the coach helps the coachee explore their existing knowledge, skills, and resources that can contribute to achieving the desired outcome. The focus is on identifying and leveraging strengths.
  Example: The coach engages the sales representative in a discussion to uncover their existing sales knowledge, skills, and experiences, such as their ability to build relationships, conduct effective presentations, or negotiate deals.
- ✓ Affirm and Action: In this step, the coach affirms the coachee's strengths, capabilities, and potential for success. The coach then helps the coachee develop specific action steps and commitments to move closer to the desired outcome.
  Example: The coach acknowledges the sales representative's strengths in building relationships and reinforces their belief in their ability to acquire major accounts. They then work together to create a plan of action that includes activities such as researching target companies, networking at industry events, and scheduling client meetings.
- ✓ Review: In this final step, the coach schedules a follow-up session to review progress, evaluate the effectiveness of the actions taken, make adjustments if necessary, and celebrate achievements.
  Example: The coach and sales representative schedule a review session after three months to assess the progress made in acquiring

major accounts, identify any challenges faced, and determine next steps based on the results achieved.

More Practical Examples using the Coaching Models

Let's expand on the GROW and OSKAR coaching models and provide practical examples for their application in various coaching scenarios.

1. GROW Model:

Goal (G):

- ✓ Coaching Scenario: A sales manager is coaching a team member who wants to increase their monthly sales target.
- ✓ Application: Begin by asking the salesperson to define their specific goal, e.g., "What is your target sales figure for the next month?"

Reality (R):

- ✓ Coaching Scenario: The salesperson assesses their current situation, identifying strengths and areas that need improvement.
- ✓ Application: The coach asks, "What is your current sales performance like? What strategies have you already used to reach your target?"

Options (O):

- ✓ Coaching Scenario: The coach encourages the salesperson to brainstorm potential solutions.
- ✓ Application: Ask, "What are some strategies or approaches you can use to increase sales? Let's list as many as possible."

Will (W):

- ✓ Coaching Scenario: The salesperson commits to an action plan and sets a timeline for achieving their goal.
- ✓ Application: Ask, "Which specific actions will you take, and by when, to reach your sales target? How can I support you?"
- ✓

2. OSKAR Model:

Outcome (O):

- ✓ Coaching Scenario: A sales manager is coaching a team member to address a performance issue.
- ✓ Application: Ask, "What is the desired outcome of this coaching session? What do you hope to achieve?"

Scaling (S):

- ✓ Coaching Scenario: The coach helps the salesperson assess their current performance on a scale of 1 to 10.
- ✓ Application: Ask, "On a scale of 1 to 10, how would you rate your current performance in terms of meeting your sales targets?"

Know-How (K):

- ✓ Coaching Scenario: The coach explores the skills, resources, and knowledge the salesperson possesses.
- ✓ Application: Ask, "What skills or knowledge do you already have that can help you improve your sales performance?"

Affirm and Action (A):

- ✓ Coaching Scenario: The coach identifies past successes and explores action steps.
- ✓ Application: Say, "Let's celebrate your past successes. Now, what are some small,

achievable steps you can take to improve your performance?"

Review (R):

- ✓ Coaching Scenario: The coach helps the salesperson reflect on their progress.
- ✓ Application: Ask, "Let's review what you've achieved and what you've learned. How can you continue to progress?"

These coaching models provide structured frameworks for sales managers to guide coaching conversations effectively. They help clarify goals, assess the current situation, explore options, and commit to actionable steps. Sales managers can choose the model that best suits the coaching scenario and the individual needs of their team members.

These models serve as effective guides to drive progress and development within the coaching relationship.

Using Technology in Coaching

The integration of technology in coaching can enhance the coaching experience and provide additional tools and resources. Here are a few ways technology can be leveraged in coaching:

- ✓ Virtual Coaching Platforms: With the rise of remote work and dispersed teams, video conferencing platforms enable coaches to conduct coaching sessions regardless of geographical locations. This technology facilitates real-time interactions and maintains a personal connection.

  Example: A sales manager coaches a team member located in a different city through a video conferencing platform, engaging in coaching conversations, providing feedback, and even utilizing screen sharing for reviewing sales presentations.

- ✓ Coaching Apps and Software: Utilizing coaching apps and software can streamline coaching processes, track progress, and provide easy access to coaching materials and resources.
  Example: A sales manager uses a coaching app to track individual sales representatives' progress, set goals, provide ongoing feedback, and access a library of sales training resources, such as videos, articles, and best practices.

By incorporating different coaching approaches, utilizing coaching models and frameworks, and leveraging technology effectively, sales managers can enhance their coaching skills and empower their team members to achieve higher levels of performance. In the next chapter, we will focus on the importance of continuous learning and development in sales coaching.

Developing Sales Skills

Effective sales skills are crucial for sales managers and their teams to achieve outstanding results. In this chapter, we will explore the process of developing sales skills through coaching. We will discuss identifying skill gaps, tailoring coaching to individual needs, and coaching for sales techniques and strategies. Specific examples will be provided to illustrate each concept effectively.

Identifying Skill Gaps

To develop sales skills effectively, it is important to identify skill gaps within the sales team. This involves assessing the current skill levels of individual team members and comparing them to the desired or required skill set. Here are some steps for identifying skill gaps:

- ✓ Conducting Skill Assessments: Sales managers can use various methods such as sales simulations, role-playing exercises, or self-assessments to evaluate the proficiency of their team members in different sales skills.
  Example: The sales manager conducts a role-playing exercise where team members engage in mock sales conversations to assess their ability to handle objections effectively.
- ✓ Analyzing Performance Data: Sales managers can analyze performance data, such as sales metrics, win rates, or customer feedback, to identify areas where their team may be falling short.
  Example: The sales manager reviews sales reports and identifies that the team struggles

with closing deals in the final stages of the sales process.

- ✓ Seeking Feedback: Sales managers can gather feedback from team members, customers, or other stakeholders to gain insights into areas where improvement is needed.

  Example: The sales manager holds one-on-one feedback sessions with each team member to gather their perspectives on their strengths and areas they feel they need to improve.

Tailoring Coaching to Individual Needs

Once skill gaps have been identified, sales managers can tailor their coaching approach to address the specific needs of each team member. This involves understanding their unique strengths, weaknesses, and learning preferences. Here are some strategies for tailoring coaching:

- ✓ Individualized Coaching Plans: Sales managers can create individualized coaching plans for each team member, focusing on the specific skills they need to develop. These plans can include targeted training, practice exercises, and regular coaching sessions.

  Example: The sales manager creates a coaching plan for a sales representative who struggles with effective prospecting techniques. The plan includes targeted training modules on prospecting, role-playing exercises, and weekly coaching sessions to review progress.
- ✓ Adapted Coaching Styles: Sales managers can adapt their coaching styles to match the preferences and learning styles of each team

member. Some may respond better to direct feedback, while others may benefit from a more collaborative approach.

Example: The sales manager recognizes that one team member prefers a collaborative coaching approach, so they engage in joint problem-solving sessions and encourage the representative to share their ideas and solutions.

Coaching for Sales Techniques and Strategies

Coaching plays a vital role in developing sales techniques and strategies that drive success. Sales managers can focus on coaching their team members on specific sales techniques, such as effective questioning, active listening, or objection handling. They can also provide guidance on sales strategies, such as account management or sales pipeline management. Here are some approaches to coaching for sales techniques and strategies:

- ✓ Skill-based Coaching: Sales managers can conduct skill-based coaching sessions where they provide targeted feedback, demonstrations, and practice opportunities to help team members refine their sales techniques.

  Example: The sales manager conducts a coaching session on active listening, providing specific examples and demonstrating active listening techniques. They then have the sales team practice active listening in mock sales conversations.
- ✓ Strategy-focused Coaching: Sales managers can provide coaching on sales strategies, helping team members develop effective approaches to various aspects of the sales

process, such as prospecting, qualifying leads, or closing deals.

Example: The sales manager holds a coaching session on effective sales prospecting strategies, sharing best practices and guiding team members in developing personalized prospecting plans based on their target markets and ideal customer profiles.

By identifying skill gaps, tailoring coaching to individual needs, and coaching for specific sales techniques and strategies, sales managers can facilitate the continuous development of their team members' sales skills. This will contribute to improved sales performance and ultimately drive the achievement of organizational goals. In the next chapter, we will delve into the importance of motivational coaching to inspire and engage sales team members.

Identifying Sales Skills Gaps using Skill Assessments

Here are more details and explanations on how to identify sales skills gaps using skill assessments:
Skill assessments are valuable tools for sales managers to evaluate the proficiency of their team members in various sales skills and identify specific areas where improvement is needed. Here's a step-by-step process for conducting skill assessments:

- ✓ Determine the Key Sales Skills: Start by identifying the key sales skills that are crucial for success in your specific sales environment. These skills may include prospecting, rapport building, effective communication, objection handling, closing deals, or account management, among others.
- ✓ Select Assessment Methods: Choose appropriate assessment methods that align with the sales skills you want to evaluate. Common methods include sales simulations, role-playing exercises, self-assessments, or even quizzes or tests focused on specific sales scenarios.
- ✓ Create Assessment Criteria: Define the criteria or benchmarks against which you will evaluate the sales skills. This could involve creating a scoring rubric or a checklist of desired behaviors and competencies.
- ✓ Conduct Assessments: Administer the skill assessments to individual team members or groups. This can be done through one-on-one sessions, team exercises, or online

assessments, depending on the nature of the assessment method chosen.

- ✓ Observe and Evaluate Performance: During the assessments, carefully observe the performance of each team member. Pay attention to their ability to demonstrate the desired sales skills, apply appropriate techniques, and achieve the desired outcomes.
- ✓ Provide Feedback and Analysis: After the assessments, provide constructive feedback to each team member based on their performance. Discuss their strengths, areas for improvement, and specific skill gaps that were identified.
- ✓ Analyze Aggregate Data: Look for patterns and trends in the assessment results across the sales team. Identify common areas of strength and weaknesses to gain insights into overall skill gaps within the team.
- ✓ Prioritize Skill Development: Based on the assessment results, prioritize the sales skills that require immediate attention and development. Focus on the skills that have the most significant impact on sales performance or align with organizational goals.
- ✓ Develop Individualized Coaching Plans: Create individualized coaching plans for each team member, addressing their specific skill gaps. Tailor the coaching plans to provide targeted training, practice exercises, and regular coaching sessions focused on developing the identified skills.
- ✓ Monitor Progress and Adjust: Continuously monitor the progress of team members as

they work on developing their sales skills. Provide ongoing support, reinforcement, and adjustments to the coaching plans as needed.

By conducting skill assessments, sales managers gain valuable insights into the strengths and weaknesses of their team members' sales skills. This enables them to focus their coaching efforts on developing the specific areas that require improvement, ultimately leading to enhanced sales performance and results.

Step by Step Process for 'Coaching Sales Techniques and Strategies'

Here's a step-by-step process for coaching sales techniques and strategies, along with specific examples:

- ✓ Step 1: Assess Individual Sales Techniques and Strategies Start by assessing the current sales techniques and strategies used by each team member. This can be done through observation, performance reviews, or self-assessments. Identify areas where improvement or refinement is needed.
  Example: During a sales call observation, you notice that a team member struggles with effective questioning techniques and fails to uncover the customer's pain points adequately.
- ✓ Step 2: Set Clear Objectives Define clear objectives for coaching sessions based on the identified areas for improvement. Ensure that the objectives are specific, measurable, achievable, relevant, and time-bound (SMART).
  Example: The objective for the coaching session might be to help the team member develop effective questioning techniques to uncover customer pain points and needs during sales conversations.
- ✓ Step 3: Provide Instruction and Demonstration Explain and demonstrate the desired sales technique or strategy to the team member.

Provide clear explanations, examples, and best practices to help them understand how to apply the technique effectively.

Example: Explain the importance of open-ended questions in sales conversations and how they can help the team member gain deeper insights into customer needs. Provide examples of effective open-ended questions and demonstrate how to use them in different sales scenarios.

✓ Step 4: Practice and Role-Play Engage in role-playing exercises to allow the team member to practice the desired sales technique or strategy. Create realistic scenarios that mirror real sales situations, and encourage the team member to apply the newly learned skills.

Example: Conduct a role-playing exercise where the team member plays the role of the salesperson, and you play the customer. Guide the conversation to focus on using open-ended questions effectively to uncover customer pain points.

✓ Step 5: Provide Feedback and Guidance Provide constructive feedback on the team member's performance during the role-play exercise. Highlight areas of improvement and offer specific suggestions for enhancing their sales technique or strategy.

Example: Provide feedback on the team member's use of open-ended questions, highlighting the strengths and areas that need improvement. Offer guidance on framing questions more effectively and probing deeper to uncover customer needs.

- ✓ Step 6: Reinforce Learning Through Application Encourage the team member to apply the newly learned sales technique or strategy in real-life sales situations. Provide ongoing support and guidance as they practice the technique and gain confidence.
  Example: Assign the team member with the task of using open-ended questions in their upcoming sales calls or meetings. Offer to review call recordings or debrief after customer interactions to provide further guidance and reinforcement.
- ✓ Step 7: Monitor Progress and Provide Continued Support Continuously monitor the team member's progress and provide ongoing support and coaching as needed. Offer additional resources, training materials, or mentoring opportunities to further develop their sales techniques and strategies.
  Example: Schedule regular check-ins with the team member to discuss their experiences applying the newly learned sales technique. Provide guidance on specific challenges they may encounter and offer additional resources, such as articles, videos, or workshops, to support their development.

By following these steps, sales managers can effectively coach their team members on sales techniques and strategies. This structured approach helps team members enhance their skills, improve their sales performance, and achieve better results.

Coaching Questions that a Sales Manager can use on a Sales Coaching Session

Here's a list of 25 coaching questions that sales managers can use during a sales coaching session:

1. *What are your top goals for this quarter or year, and how can I support you in achieving them?*
2. *What specific challenges or obstacles are you currently facing in your sales efforts?*
3. *Can you describe a recent successful sale? What do you think contributed to that success?*
4. *What strategies have you found effective in building rapport with potential clients or customers?*
5. *Are there any particular objections or concerns that you encounter frequently during your sales calls? How do you handle them?*
6. *How well do you understand the unique needs and pain points of your customers? Can you share an example of how you've addressed these effectively?*
7. *What sales techniques or methods do you feel most comfortable using, and which ones do you find more challenging?*
8. *Can you walk me through your sales process, from the initial contact with a lead to closing the deal?*
9. *Are there any areas of the sales process where you feel you could use additional training or guidance?*

10. *What's your approach to setting and achieving your sales targets or quotas?*
11. *How do you prioritize and manage your leads or clients to ensure a balanced and effective sales pipeline?*
12. *Do you feel that your time management and organization skills are supporting your sales efforts, or is there room for improvement?*
13. *How do you typically prepare for a sales meeting or call? Are there specific strategies or tools you find most helpful?*
14. *Can you share a recent situation where you encountered resistance from a potential customer? How did you handle it, and what did you learn from the experience?*
15. *What strategies do you use to keep your sales presentations or pitches engaging and persuasive?*
16. *How do you measure your own success and evaluate your performance as a salesperson?*
17. *Are there any specific areas of self-improvement you'd like to focus on to become a more effective salesperson?*
18. *Can you provide examples of how you build and maintain long-term relationships with your clients or customers?*
19. *What role does active listening play in your sales process, and how do you ensure you're fully understanding your customers' needs?*
20. *How do you handle rejection or deals that don't close? What strategies do you use to stay motivated?*
21. *Are there particular products or services in your portfolio that you feel less confident*

selling? How can I help you improve in those areas?

22. *How do you leverage technology or tools to support your sales efforts, such as CRM systems or sales analytics?*
23. *Can you share a specific sales scenario or challenge you'd like to role-play or discuss during this coaching session?*
24. *What are your personal and professional development goals, and how can we align your coaching with these objectives?*
25. *What can I, as your sales manager, do to support your growth and success in the sales role?*

These coaching questions are designed to guide productive discussions during sales coaching sessions and help sales professionals reflect on their performance and areas of improvement.

Role-Playing Scenarios

Here are detailed role-playing scenarios with sample dialogues and coaching interactions to help sales managers practice their coaching skills. These scenarios cover various coaching situations and offer guidance on how to conduct effective coaching sessions, offering practical examples of how sales managers can guide their sales teams in various sales situations. They allow sales managers to practice coaching techniques and provide feedback for skill development.

Scenario 1: Developing Prospecting Skills

Role-play: The sales manager is coaching a salesperson on effective prospecting.

Salesperson: *"I'm struggling to identify high-potential leads. How can I improve my prospecting?"*

Sales Manager (Coach): *"Great question. Let's practice creating an ideal customer profile together."*

Salesperson: *"I think our ideal customer is a small business owner with a need for cost-effective solutions."*

Sales Manager (Coach): *"Good start. Now, let's create a prospecting script that resonates with this profile. Role-play initiating a prospecting call."*

Salesperson: *"Hello, I'm calling to introduce our cost-effective solutions for small business owners like you..."*

Sales Manager (Coach): *"Good script. Let's now discuss your approach to nurturing leads. How can you build relationships with these prospects over time?"*

Continue the role-play with the salesperson developing a lead nurturing strategy.

Scenario 2: Handling Customer Objections

Role-play: The sales manager is coaching a salesperson on handling objections from a potential customer.

Salesperson: *"I'm interested in your product, but it seems a bit expensive."*

Sales Manager (Coach): "Great job in getting the prospect interested. Now, let's address the objection. Ask them to clarify their concerns."

Salesperson: *"Can you tell me more about what or why you find it expensive?"*

Sales Manager (Coach): *"Excellent. Now, use the 'Feel-Felt-Found' technique to empathize and provide a solution."*

Salesperson: "*I understand how you feel. Many of our customers have felt the same way initially. However, what they found is that our product provides exceptional value because..."*

Sales Manager (Coach): *"Good start. Remember to highlight the specific benefits and ROI. Let's practice that."*

Continue the role-play with the salesperson elaborating on product benefits and the customer's likely response.

Scenario 3: Closing the Sale

Role-play: The sales manager is coaching a salesperson on closing a deal.

Salesperson: *"I've explained our product features and benefits, and the prospect seems interested. What should I do next?"*

Sales Manager (Coach): *"Good progress. Now, let's practice using the 'Alternative Choice' closing technique."*
Salesperson: *"Would you like to move forward with the standard package, or would our premium package better suit your needs?"*
Sales Manager (Coach): *"Nice job using the alternative choice. Now, be prepared for their response and handle objections if needed."*
Continue the role-play with the salesperson addressing the customer's choice and potential objections.

Scenario 4: Post-Sale Customer Follow-Up
Role-play: The sales manager is coaching a salesperson on post-sale customer follow-up.
Salesperson: *"I'm unsure about the right way to follow up with customers after a sale. What should I do?"*
Sales Manager (Coach): *"Excellent question. Let's role-play a post-sale follow-up call."*
Salesperson: *"I wanted to check in and see how you're finding our product..."*
Sales Manager (Coach): *"Good start. Now, remember to express gratitude and ask for referrals during the call."*
Salesperson: *"I also wanted to thank you for choosing our product. Do you know anyone else who might benefit from it?"*
Sales Manager (Coach): *"Great job incorporating referrals. Let's discuss a strategy for handling common post-sale issues."*
Continue the role-play with the salesperson addressing potential post-sale issues and providing solutions.

Example of a Coaching Plan and Schedule

Creating a comprehensive coaching plan and schedule using the 8-step sales model can be a valuable tool for sales managers. Here's a detailed coaching plan with examples for each step of the model:

Coaching Plan and Schedule

Sales Model: The 8-Step Sales Process

1. Preparing:

Objective: To ensure that salespeople are well-prepared for every customer interaction.

Coaching Activities:

- ✓ Review and update product knowledge, uncovering needs questions, and list of product benefits and sales materials to carry.
- ✓ Set objectives and goals for upcoming customer interactions.
- ✓ Example: The sales manager conducts a weekly product knowledge session where the team learns about new products and competitors' offerings. They also discuss questions to uncover needs and product benefits, including common customer objections and practice objection handling.

2. Prospecting:

Objective: To identify and prioritize potential leads and prospects effectively.

Coaching Activities:

- ✓ Review lead generation strategies and sources.
- ✓ Share best practices for identifying high-potential leads.

- ✓ Example: The manager provides guidance on using CRM software to track and manage leads. They discuss different prospecting techniques, such as cold calling, email marketing, and social media outreach.

3. Approaching:

Objective: To make a strong and engaging initial impression on prospects.

Coaching Activities:

- ✓ Role-play approach and opening lines.
- ✓ Provide feedback on body language, tone, and attitude.
- ✓ Example: The sales manager conducts role-playing exercises where team members practice their approach and receive feedback. They emphasize the importance of active listening and building rapport.

4. Uncovering Needs:

Objective: To understand the specific needs and pain points of the prospect.

Coaching Activities:

- ✓ Discuss effective questioning techniques.
- ✓ Review the importance of empathy and active listening.
- ✓ Example: The manager highlights the significance of open-ended questions to uncover customer needs. They share a success story where a salesperson effectively used probing questions to identify a prospect's unique challenges.

5. Proving Value and Selling Benefits:

Objective: To demonstrate the value of the product or service and its benefits.

Coaching Activities:

- ✓ Analyze product features and benefits.

- ✓ Share successful case studies and value propositions.
- ✓ Example: The manager conducts a product features and benefits workshop, providing real-world examples of how the product has solved problems for previous customers.

6. Recommending and Presenting:

Objective: To recommend a tailored solution and present it effectively.

Coaching Activities:

- ✓ Discuss the importance of tailored solutions.
- ✓ Provide guidelines for creating persuasive presentations.
- ✓ Example: The manager reviews a recent presentation by a team member, offering feedback on areas where they effectively tailored the solution to the prospect's needs and where improvements can be made.

7. Closing with Add-ons/Cross-Selling:

Objective: To close the deal and explore opportunities for up-selling or cross-selling.

Coaching Activities:

- ✓ Discuss various closing techniques.
- ✓ Share successful up-sell and cross-sell scenarios.
- ✓ Example: The manager conducts a session on closing techniques, emphasizing the importance of creating a sense of urgency. They share a success story where a salesperson up-sold additional services by highlighting their value to the customer.

8. After Sales Service:

Objective: To ensure customers receive excellent post-sale service and support.

Coaching Activities:

- ✓ Discuss strategies for building long-term customer relationships.
- ✓ Role-play post-sale customer interactions.
- ✓ Example: The manager emphasizes the importance of post-sale follow-ups and shares a situation where a salesperson resolved a post-sale issue promptly, leading to increased customer satisfaction and referrals.

Coaching Schedule:

- ✓ Daily: 15-minute check-ins for progress updates and immediate feedback.
- ✓ Weekly: 1-hour training sessions focusing on a specific step in the sales process.
- ✓ Bi-weekly: 1-on-1 coaching sessions for personalized feedback and goal setting.
- ✓ Monthly: Review of individual and team performance, with an emphasis on continuous improvement and goal adjustment.

This coaching plan and schedule ensure that the sales team is well-prepared, knowledgeable, and skilled at each step of the sales process. It promotes continuous learning and development, improving sales performance and customer satisfaction.

Sample Format to Monitor and Evaluate Coaching Sessions

Here's a detailed format that a sales manager can use to monitor and evaluate coaching sessions with sales team members. This format includes areas of evaluation and grading for each section.

Coaching Session: Monitoring and Evaluation Form

Coaching Session Date: [Date]
Salesperson's Name: [Salesperson's Name]
Coach's Name (Sales Manager): [Coach's Name]

I. Preparation and Goal Setting:
Clarity of Objectives (1-5):
1: Objectives were unclear or not discussed.
2: Objectives were somewhat clear.
3: Objectives were adequately clear.
4: Objectives were very clear.
5: Objectives were exceptionally clear.
Preparation and Research (1-5):
1: Minimal preparation and research.
2: Limited preparation and research.
3: Moderate preparation and research.
4: Good preparation and research.
5: Excellent preparation and research.

II. Coaching Session Effectiveness:
Active Listening (1-5):
1: Poor active listening; frequent interruptions.
2: Limited active listening; occasional interruptions.
3: Adequate active listening; few interruptions.

4: Good active listening; minimal interruptions.
5: Excellent active listening; no interruptions.

Feedback Delivery (1-5):

1: Ineffective feedback; too critical.
2: Feedback needs improvement; somewhat critical.
3: Adequate feedback; balanced.
4: Effective feedback; constructive.
5: Exceptional feedback; highly constructive.

Questioning Techniques (1-5):

1: Poor questioning; lack of open-ended questions.
2: Limited questioning; few open-ended questions.
3: Adequate questioning; some open-ended questions.
4: Good questioning; effective use of open-ended questions.
5: Excellent questioning; frequent, insightful open-ended questions.

III. Coaching Content and Strategy:

Alignment with Sales Goals (1-5):

1: Coaching content had no alignment with sales goals.
2: Limited alignment with sales goals.
3: Adequate alignment with sales goals.
4: Good alignment with sales goals.
5: Excellent alignment with sales goals.

Skill Development (1-5):

1: Ineffective skill development; no clear focus.
2: Skill development needs improvement; limited focus.
3: Adequate skill development; some focus.
4: Effective skill development; clear focus.
5: Exceptional skill development; highly focused.

Goal Setting and Action Plan (1-5):

1: Vague or non-existent goals and action plans.

2: Goals and action plans need improvement; somewhat clear.
3: Adequate goals and action plans; moderately clear.
4: Clear and effective goals and action plans.
5: Exceptional goals and action plans; highly clear and actionable.

IV. Relationship Building:

Rapport Building (1-5):

1: Poor rapport building; minimal efforts.
2: Limited rapport building; some efforts.
3: Adequate rapport building; moderate efforts.
4: Good rapport building; substantial efforts.
5: Excellent rapport building; strong efforts.

V. Overall Coaching Session:

Overall Effectiveness (1-5):
1: Highly ineffective coaching session.
2: Ineffective coaching session.
3: Moderately effective coaching session.
4: Effective coaching session.
5: Highly effective coaching session.

VI. Additional Comments and Recommendations:

[Provide specific comments, observations, and recommendations for improvement.]

Coach's Signature: ______________________________
Salesperson's Signature:________________________

This detailed form allows the sales manager to objectively assess various aspects of the coaching session, providing feedback that is specific and actionable. It helps ensure that the coaching process is constructive and focused on the improvement of sales team members.

Managing Remote Sales Teams: Strategies and Best Practices for Coaching Success

In a rapidly evolving work landscape, the way sales teams operate has transformed dramatically. With the rise of remote and virtual sales teams, effective coaching is more essential than ever. In this chapter, we'll explore strategies and best practices for coaching remote sales teams, ensuring that they remain motivated, engaged, and successful in a virtual environment.

The New Reality of Remote Sales Teams

In recent years, the sales landscape has shifted. Remote and virtual sales teams have become a new reality. This section discusses the challenges and opportunities presented by remote sales teams.

Challenges of Remote Sales Teams:

- ✓ Lack of In-Person Interaction: Sales teams miss out on the spontaneous exchanges and feedback that happen in a physical office setting.
- ✓ Isolation and Motivation: Team members may struggle with isolation, potentially affecting their motivation and job satisfaction.
- ✓ Communication Hurdles: Remote teams rely heavily on technology for communication, which can sometimes lead to misunderstandings or miscommunication.

Opportunities of Remote Sales Teams:

- ✓ Wider Talent Pool: Organizations can tap into a global talent pool, potentially finding sales talent that wasn't accessible before.

- ✓ Flexibility: Salespeople can manage their work in a way that suits their lifestyles, potentially improving work-life balance.
- ✓ Cost Savings: Reduced office space and infrastructure costs can lead to savings.

Strategies for Effective Remote Sales Coaching

This section outlines strategies for sales managers to effectively coach remote teams, ensuring that they remain motivated and productive.

1. Clear Communication:
   - ✓ Strategy: Prioritize clear, frequent, and multi-modal communication. Use video calls, messaging platforms, and emails.
   - ✓ Example: Schedule regular video meetings to maintain face-to-face interactions. Use chat tools for quick updates and queries.
2. Goal Alignment:
   - ✓ Strategy: Ensure that remote sales team members' individual goals align with the organization's objectives.
   - ✓ Example: In a coaching session, discuss how the salesperson's goals contribute to the team's and the company's success.
3. Structured Coaching Sessions:
   - ✓ Strategy: Maintain a regular schedule of coaching sessions, even when working remotely.
   - ✓ Example: Have weekly coaching sessions at the same time to create a sense of consistency.
4. Monitoring and Accountability:
   - ✓ Strategy: Use technology to monitor performance and hold remote team members accountable.

- ✓ Example: Implement CRM software to track sales activities, progress, and goals.

Best Practices for Coaching Remote Sales Teams

This section delves into best practices that sales managers can put into practice when coaching remote sales teams.

1. Empathy and Support:
   - ✓ Best Practice: Show empathy and provide emotional support during coaching sessions.
   - ✓ Example: Begin coaching sessions by asking how the salesperson is feeling and if they face any challenges outside of work.
2. Feedback Loops:
   - ✓ Best Practice: Establish a structured system for feedback and evaluation.
   - ✓ Example: Provide weekly feedback and conduct quarterly performance reviews to ensure a consistent feedback loop.
3. Individualization:
   - ✓ Best Practice: Recognize that remote team members have individual needs and adapt coaching accordingly.
   - ✓ Example: Tailor coaching sessions to address the unique challenges or strengths of each salesperson.
4. Virtual Training and Resources:
   - ✓ Best Practice: Provide access to virtual training resources and tools for skill development.
   - ✓ Example: Offer online training modules or subscriptions to industry publications for continued learning.

Real-World Success Stories

In this section, we share real-world success stories from organizations that have effectively managed remote sales teams, highlighting their strategies and outcomes.

Success Story 1: XYZ Corporation

- ✓ Strategy: XYZ Corporation implemented regular virtual team-building exercises to foster collaboration among their remote sales team. This resulted in increased team cohesion and improved performance.

Success Story 2: ABC Solutions

- ✓ Strategy: ABC Solutions leveraged technology to monitor and provide instant feedback to their remote sales team members. This improved individual and team performance, leading to record sales numbers.

As seen, managing remote sales teams requires a unique approach. Effective coaching, clear communication, and tailored support are crucial for success.

By applying these strategies and best practices, sales managers can ensure that their remote sales teams remain motivated, engaged, and successful in the evolving work landscape. The key is to adapt to the changing environment while maintaining a focus on individual and team development.

Handling Sales Personnel Attitude and Habits for Improved Performance

We will now delve into the crucial aspects of addressing and coaching sales personnel whose attitudes or habits may be affecting their performance. We'll discuss how to identify such issues, understand their impact, and implement effective coaching strategies.

Identifying Attitude and Habit Issues

Signs of Attitude Problems

Identifying attitude issues in sales personnel often requires a keen observation of behavior and communication. Signs of attitude problems may include:

- ✓ **Negativity**: Consistently expressing pessimism or cynicism.
- ✓ **Resentment**: Showing resistance to tasks or colleagues.
- ✓ **Defensiveness**: Reacting to feedback with defensiveness.
- ✓ **Lack of Accountability**: Not taking responsibility for mistakes.
- ✓ **Lack of Enthusiasm**: A general lack of enthusiasm or motivation.

Recognizing Habitual Behavior

Identifying problematic habits can be equally important for coaching success. Some signs of detrimental habits include:

- ✓ **Procrastination**: Consistently delaying important tasks.

- ✓ **Ineffective Time Management**: Poorly managing time and tasks.
- ✓ **Over-reliance on Comfort Zones**: Avoiding challenges.
- ✓ **Inconsistent Follow-Up**: Failing to follow up with leads or clients.
- ✓ **Inefficient Planning**: Poor planning that leads to disorganized work.

Understanding the Impact

Impact of Attitude Problems

Addressing attitude problems is crucial because they can significantly impact sales performance and team dynamics:

- ✓ **Reduced Morale**: Negative attitudes can spread and lower team morale.
- ✓ **Customer Interactions**: Negative attitudes can affect client relationships.
- ✓ **Decreased Productivity**: Pessimism can hinder performance.

Impact of Habits

Ineffective habits can also have a direct impact on sales performance:

- ✓ **Missed Opportunities**: Poor time management can lead to missed sales opportunities.
- ✓ **Inconsistent Results**: Inefficient habits may lead to inconsistent performance.
- ✓ **Reduced Confidence**: Failing to address bad habits can erode confidence.

Coaching Strategies

Coaching Attitude Problems

Coaching sales personnel with attitude problems requires a structured approach:

Example Scenario: A salesperson displays a consistently negative attitude, impacting team morale.

- ✓ **Open Dialogue**: Initiate a conversation to understand the source of negativity.
- ✓ **Set Clear Expectations**: Define expectations for attitude and behavior.
- ✓ **Provide Feedback**: Offer specific feedback and share the impact of their attitude.
- ✓ **Goal Setting**: Collaboratively set goals for attitude improvement.
- ✓ **Mentoring**: Pair the salesperson with a mentor or coach for ongoing support.

Coaching Habitual Behavior

Addressing poor habits demands a different approach:

Example Scenario: A salesperson consistently procrastinates in following up with leads.

- ✓ **Identify the Habit**: Clearly identify the problematic habit (procrastination).
- ✓ **Set SMART Goals**: Establish Specific, Measurable, Achievable, Relevant, and Time-bound goals.
- ✓ **Training and Skill Development**: Offer training on time management and productivity.
- ✓ **Create Accountability**: Set up accountability measures to track habit change.
- ✓ **Positive Reinforcement**: Acknowledge and reward improvements in habit.

Case Studies

Case Study 1: Attitude Transformation

- ✓ **Scenario**: A salesperson with a consistently negative attitude improved after coaching.

- ✓ **Approach**: Through open dialogue, goal setting, and continuous mentoring, the salesperson's attitude transformed. The impact was a more positive work environment and improved team morale.

Case Study 2: Habit Overhaul

- ✓ **Scenario**: A salesperson who habitually procrastinated in follow-ups improved.
- ✓ **Approach**: By identifying the habit, setting SMART goals, providing training, creating accountability, and offering positive reinforcement, the salesperson overcame procrastination. This resulted in more consistent and successful follow-ups, leading to increased sales.

Addressing attitude and habit issues in sales personnel is critical for improving their performance. By identifying these issues, understanding their impact, and applying effective coaching strategies, sales managers can empower their team members to reach their full potential and contribute to the organization's success. Remember that attitude and habits can change with the right coaching and support, leading to improved sales outcomes.

Motivating and Inspiring Sales Teams

Motivation plays a crucial role in driving sales team performance and achieving sales targets. In this chapter, we will explore strategies for motivating and inspiring sales teams. We will discuss understanding motivation factors, building a motivating environment, and using incentives and recognition. Specific examples will be provided to illustrate each concept effectively.

Understanding Motivation Factors

To effectively motivate sales teams, it is essential to understand the factors that drive motivation. Different individuals are motivated by different factors, so sales managers should consider the following:

- ✓ Recognition and Achievement: Many sales professionals are motivated by recognition for their achievements. Acknowledging their accomplishments, both privately and publicly, can fuel their motivation.

  Example: A sales manager holds a monthly team meeting where outstanding performers are recognized and celebrated in front of the entire team. This recognition reinforces their sense of achievement and motivates others to strive for similar recognition.
- ✓ Personal and Professional Growth: Salespeople often value opportunities for personal and professional growth. Providing avenues for skill development, career advancement, and learning can fuel their motivation.

Example: The sales manager offers sales training programs, industry certifications, or workshops to enhance the team's skills and knowledge. They also provide opportunities for team members to attend conferences or industry events to expand their professional network.

- ✓ Autonomy and Ownership: Granting sales team members autonomy and ownership over their work can be a powerful motivator. Allowing them to make decisions, set goals, and take ownership of their sales processes can foster motivation.

  Example: The sales manager empowers sales representatives to create their own sales strategies, set ambitious goals, and make decisions regarding their sales approach. This autonomy fosters a sense of ownership and motivates them to take responsibility for their performance.

Building a Motivating Environment

Creating a motivating environment is crucial for inspiring sales teams. The work environment should be supportive, positive, and conducive to high performance. Consider the following strategies:

- ✓ Open Communication: Foster an environment of open and transparent communication where team members feel comfortable expressing their ideas, concerns, and feedback.

  Example: The sales manager holds regular team meetings, one-on-one sessions, or utilizes communication tools such as chat platforms to encourage open dialogue and information sharing.

- ✓ Collaboration and Teamwork: Promote a collaborative culture where team members support and help each other. Encourage knowledge sharing, idea generation, and teamwork to foster a sense of camaraderie.
  Example: The sales manager organizes team-building activities, encourages cross-team collaboration, and facilitates knowledge-sharing sessions where successful sales techniques or strategies are shared among team members.
- ✓ Positive Reinforcement: Provide positive feedback, encouragement, and support to boost morale and motivation within the team.
  Example: The sales manager regularly praises team members for their hard work, provides constructive feedback on areas of improvement, and offers support and resources to help them succeed.

Using Incentives and Recognition

Incentives and recognition programs can be powerful motivators for sales teams. By rewarding exceptional performance, sales managers can inspire and drive their team members to achieve their best. Consider the following approaches:

- ✓ Performance-based Incentives: Design incentive programs that reward sales team members based on their individual or team performance. These incentives can be financial or non-financial rewards.
  Example: The sales manager implements a quarterly sales contest where top performers are rewarded with bonuses, gift cards, or even experiential rewards like a paid vacation or attending a conference.

- ✓ Sales Leaderboards: Create visual sales leaderboards or dashboards to publicly display individual and team performance. This fosters healthy competition and motivates team members to strive for higher rankings.

  Example: The sales manager utilizes a sales performance tracking tool that displays real-time leaderboards in the office or on a shared digital platform. Team members can see their rankings, creating a sense of competition and motivation.
- ✓ Peer Recognition Programs: Implement peer recognition programs where team members can nominate and recognize each other for exceptional performance, teamwork, or other commendable actions.

  Example: The sales manager introduces a "Sales Star of the Month" program where team members nominate their peers for outstanding contributions. The selected individual receives public recognition and a special reward.

By understanding motivation factors, building a motivating environment, and utilizing incentives and recognition, sales managers can effectively motivate and inspire their sales teams. These strategies create an atmosphere of enthusiasm, drive, and continuous improvement, leading to enhanced sales performance and success.

Overcoming Challenges in Sales Coaching

Sales coaching can sometimes present challenges for sales managers. In this chapter, we will explore strategies for overcoming these challenges. We will discuss resistance to coaching, dealing with difficult conversations, and handling underperforming salespeople. Specific examples will be provided to illustrate each scenario effectively.

Resistance to Coaching

Resistance to coaching can occur when sales team members are hesitant or reluctant to engage in the coaching process. Overcoming this resistance requires a thoughtful approach and effective communication. Consider the following strategies:

- ✓ Understanding the Resistance: Take the time to understand the underlying reasons for the resistance. It could be due to a lack of trust, fear of judgment, or a perceived threat to their autonomy.

  Example: A sales representative might resist coaching because they fear that their weaknesses will be exposed and impact their performance evaluations. Understanding this fear allows the sales manager to address it proactively.

  Building Trust: Build a trusting relationship with the sales team member by demonstrating empathy, active listening, and confidentiality. Assure them that coaching is intended to support their growth and development.

  Example: The sales manager holds regular one-on-one sessions with the sales representative, actively listens to their concerns, and assures them that coaching discussions will remain confidential.

- ✓ Explaining the Benefits: Clearly communicate the benefits of coaching, emphasizing how it can enhance their skills, boost their performance, and contribute to their long-term success.
  Example: The sales manager explains to the sales representative how coaching can help them improve their sales techniques, increase their confidence, and achieve their sales targets more consistently.

Dealing with Difficult Conversations

Difficult conversations are inevitable in sales coaching, especially when addressing performance issues or providing critical feedback. Handling these conversations effectively is crucial to maintaining a positive and productive coaching relationship. Consider the following strategies:

- ✓ Prepare and Plan: Before the conversation, prepare by outlining key points, facts, and specific examples to support your feedback. Plan for a private and comfortable setting to ensure a focused and respectful conversation.
  Example: The sales manager prepares for a conversation with a sales representative who has been consistently missing their sales targets. They gather sales data, review specific deals, and note areas where improvement is needed.
- ✓ Use the SBI (Situation-Behavior-Impact) Model: Structure the conversation using the SBI model, where you describe the specific

situation, the observed behavior, and the impact it has on performance or the team.

Example: The sales manager addresses a situation where a sales representative has been consistently arriving late for team meetings (situation). They explain that the behavior is disruptive and affects team collaboration and communication (behavior) and that it undermines the team's efficiency and morale (impact).

- ✓ Active Listening and Empathy: Practice active listening to understand the sales representative's perspective and demonstrate empathy. Allow them to express their thoughts and feelings, and show understanding of their challenges.

  Example: The sales manager listens attentively to the sales representative's explanation for the underperformance, acknowledges their frustrations, and empathizes with the difficulties they may have faced.

Handling Underperforming Salespeople

Managing underperforming salespeople can be challenging, but it is essential for maintaining team effectiveness and achieving sales targets. Here are strategies for handling underperforming salespeople:

- ✓ Identify Root Causes: Investigate the underlying reasons for the underperformance, whether it's a lack of skills, insufficient motivation, or external factors. Identify the specific areas where improvement is needed.

  Example: The sales manager determines that an underperforming salesperson is struggling with objection handling and lacks confidence in presenting the value proposition to clients.

- ✓ Individualized Development Plans: Create individualized development plans for underperforming salespeople, focusing on targeted skill development and providing support and resources for improvement.

  Example: The sales manager designs a development plan for the salesperson, including targeted training sessions on objection handling techniques and regular practice sessions to build confidence in presenting the value proposition.

- ✓ Ongoing Monitoring and Support: Continuously monitor the progress of underperforming salespeople, provide regular feedback, and offer additional coaching and support as needed.

  Example: The sales manager schedules weekly check-ins with the salesperson to review their progress, offer guidance on specific challenges, and provide ongoing support and motivation.

By implementing strategies to address resistance to coaching, handle difficult conversations, and manage underperforming salespeople, sales managers can overcome challenges effectively. This promotes a culture of continuous improvement, fosters positive working relationships, and maximizes the potential of the sales team.

Handling Coaching Resistance from Sales Personnel

Sales personnel may resist coaching sessions for various reasons, and it's essential for a sales manager to handle each situation with understanding, empathy, and effective strategies. Here are common reasons for resistance and ways to address them:

1. Fear of Criticism:
   - ✓ Handling: Emphasize that coaching is a supportive and constructive process. Encourage open communication and a non-judgmental environment where feedback is aimed at improvement, not criticism.
2. Time Constraints:
   - ✓ Handling: Respect their time. Schedule coaching sessions during less busy periods, and keep them concise and focused. Highlight the long-term time savings that can result from improved skills.
3. Lack of Relevance:
   - ✓ Handling: Ensure coaching is tailored to their specific needs and challenges. Highlight how coaching can directly address the issues they face in their day-to-day work.
4. Perceived Self-Sufficiency:
   - ✓ Handling: Discuss the benefits of continuous improvement. Share success stories of high-performing salespeople who continue to seek coaching for ongoing growth.
5. Resistance to Change:
   - ✓ Handling: Acknowledge the discomfort of change but emphasize that growth and

adaptability are critical for success. Highlight the potential for increased earnings and career advancement through coaching.

6. Low Self-Esteem or Confidence:
   - ✓ Handling: Provide emotional support and encouragement. Focus on building their self-confidence and reassure them that coaching is designed to help them overcome challenges.
7. Skepticism About Coaching's Value:
   - ✓ Handling: Share data and success stories of other team members who have benefited from coaching. Explain the direct correlation between coaching and performance improvement.
8. Discomfort with Vulnerability:
   - ✓ Handling: Create a safe and confidential space for coaching. Emphasize that vulnerability is a strength when it leads to personal and professional growth.
9. Lack of Trust in the Coach:
   - ✓ Handling: Build trust through open and honest communication. Share your expertise and success as a sales manager and coach. Be consistent in your support.
10. Resistance to Technology:
    - ✓ Handling: Provide training and support to help them navigate any technology or tools used in coaching. Show how these tools can simplify their work and improve results.
11. Overemphasis on Metrics:
    - ✓ Handling: Balance the coaching conversation by discussing both soft skills and hard metrics. Show how improved skills can translate into better metrics.

12. Fear of Failure:
    - ✓ Handling: Emphasize that coaching is a safe space for learning and that failures are opportunities for growth. Share stories of successful people who've faced setbacks.
13. Resistance to Role-Playing:
    - ✓ Handling: Explain the value of role-playing in skill development. Encourage them to view it as a low-risk practice ground where mistakes are opportunities for improvement.
14. Unwillingness to Collaborate:
    - ✓ Handling: Highlight that coaching is a collaborative process, not a top-down directive. Emphasize that their input and ideas are valued and encouraged.
15. External Stressors:
    - ✓ Handling: Be understanding of personal challenges and offer flexibility in coaching schedules. Encourage them to discuss and seek support for personal stressors.
16. Burnout:
    - ✓ Handling: Recognize signs of burnout and provide resources for self-care. Suggest adjustments to workload and discuss how coaching can help manage stress.
17. Ego and Arrogance:
    - ✓ Handling: Use data and results to humbly demonstrate areas for improvement. Encourage them to view coaching as an opportunity to refine their already strong skills.
18. Unwillingness to Self-Reflect:
    - ✓ Handling: Discuss the importance of self-reflection in personal and professional growth. Share techniques for effective self-reflection.
19. Lack of Motivation:

- ✓ Handling: Identify their intrinsic and extrinsic motivators. Help them set personal and career goals and show how coaching can help achieve them.

20. Insecurity about Job Security:
    - ✓ Handling: Assure them that coaching is an investment in their job security and career growth. Highlight how enhanced skills make them more valuable to the organization.

Handling resistance to coaching requires a mix of empathy, communication, and demonstrating the clear value of coaching in terms of personal and professional growth. It's important to address each individual's concerns and motivations to create a coaching relationship based on trust and mutual benefit.

Dealing with Difficult Conversations

Dealing with difficult conversations in sales coaching requires careful handling to address performance issues or provide critical feedback while maintaining a positive and productive coaching relationship. Here are more details and specific examples to illustrate effective approaches:

- ✓ Prepare and Plan: Before initiating a difficult conversation, take the time to prepare and plan for it. This includes outlining key points, gathering relevant data or examples, and considering the specific behaviors or situations that need to be addressed. Planning allows you to approach the conversation with clarity and confidence.

  Example: Let's say you need to address a sales representative's persistent lack of follow-up with leads. Before the conversation, you collect data on missed opportunities, incomplete follow-up actions, and customer feedback.
- ✓ Use the SBI (Situation-Behavior-Impact) Model: The SBI model is a valuable framework for structuring difficult conversations. It involves describing the specific situation, the observed behavior, and the impact it has on performance or the team. This framework provides a clear structure and helps to focus the conversation on facts and outcomes.

  Example: In discussing the sales representative's lack of follow-up, you can explain the situation by mentioning specific instances where leads were not contacted promptly or where follow-up actions were incomplete. Then, describe the behavior by pointing out the consistent pattern of missed opportunities or incomplete follow-up tasks. Finally, highlight the impact of this behavior, such as lost sales opportunities or customer dissatisfaction.

- ✓ Active Listening and Empathy: Difficult conversations require active listening and demonstrating empathy towards the sales representative's perspective. Show genuine interest in their point of view and provide them with a safe space to express their thoughts, concerns, or challenges. This helps build trust and fosters open communication.

  Example: During the conversation, actively listen to the sales representative's explanations for their lack of follow-up. Allow them to share their challenges, such as being overwhelmed with other tasks or facing difficulties in managing their time effectively. Validate their perspective and demonstrate empathy by acknowledging their frustrations and recognizing the obstacles they may be facing.

- ✓ Focus on Solutions and Improvement: While addressing performance issues, it is important to maintain a solution-oriented mindset. Emphasize the importance of finding ways to improve performance rather than dwelling on past mistakes or shortcomings. Collaborate with the sales representative to identify actionable steps for improvement.

Example: After discussing the issue of inconsistent follow-up, shift the conversation towards finding solutions. Work together with the sales representative to identify potential strategies for better time management, prioritize follow-up tasks, or utilize tools or resources that can aid in efficient lead tracking and follow-up.

- ✓ Establish Clear Expectations and Support: Conclude the difficult conversation by establishing clear expectations moving forward. Clearly communicate the desired changes or improvements and outline the support and resources that will be provided to assist the sales representative in meeting these expectations.

  Example: Summarize the expectations for improved follow-up practices, such as responding to leads within a specific timeframe or completing follow-up actions promptly. Offer ongoing support, such as additional training on time management or providing tools that streamline the lead tracking process.

By following these strategies, sales managers can navigate difficult conversations effectively, address performance issues, and guide sales representatives towards improvement. This approach promotes open dialogue, maintains positive relationships, and contributes to the overall growth and success of the sales team.

Handling Underperforming Salespeople

Handling underperforming salespeople requires a thoughtful and proactive approach to address performance issues and help them improve. Here are more details and specific examples to illustrate effective strategies:

- ✓ Identify Root Causes: When dealing with underperforming salespeople, it is essential to identify the underlying reasons for their performance issues. This involves understanding whether the underperformance stems from a lack of skills, low motivation, external factors, or other challenges. Identifying the root causes helps you tailor your coaching approach accordingly.
  Example: Let's say you have a salesperson who consistently fails to meet their sales targets. After analyzing their performance and conducting discussions, you determine that the root cause is their difficulty in handling objections during sales conversations.
- ✓ Individualized Development Plans: Once you have identified the specific areas for improvement, create individualized development plans for underperforming salespeople. These plans outline targeted actions, goals, and resources needed to support their growth and help them succeed.
  Example: For the salesperson struggling with objection handling, you can design a development plan that includes targeted training sessions on objection handling

techniques, providing them with relevant resources, and offering opportunities for practice and feedback.

- ✓ Ongoing Monitoring and Support: Regularly monitor the progress of underperforming salespeople and provide ongoing support to help them stay on track. This includes offering feedback, guidance, and additional coaching as needed. Be proactive in checking in with them and providing assistance to ensure they are supported throughout the improvement process.

  Example: Schedule weekly check-ins with the underperforming salesperson to review their progress, discuss any challenges they are facing, and offer guidance on specific areas of improvement. Provide constructive feedback on their performance, highlighting both their strengths and areas where further development is needed.
- ✓ Goal Setting and Tracking: Set specific goals and milestones to track the progress of underperforming salespeople. These goals should be achievable, measurable, and aligned with overall sales objectives. Regularly review their performance against these goals to provide feedback and support their improvement journey.

  Example: Set a goal for the salesperson to increase their conversion rate by a certain percentage within a specified timeframe. Track their conversion rate regularly, provide feedback on their progress, and discuss strategies to improve their performance.

- ✓ Coaching and Skill Development: Offer targeted coaching and skill development opportunities to underperforming salespeople. This can involve role-playing exercises, shadowing successful team members, or providing access to sales training programs. Tailor the coaching approach to address their specific needs and challenges.
  Example: Arrange role-playing sessions where the underperforming salesperson can practice objection handling techniques with a more experienced colleague. Provide constructive feedback and guidance on their performance to help them refine their skills.
- ✓ Positive Reinforcement and Recognition: Alongside constructive feedback, provide positive reinforcement and recognition to underperforming salespeople when they make progress or achieve milestones. Celebrate their successes and acknowledge their efforts, as it can enhance motivation and boost their confidence.
  Example: Publicly recognize the salesperson's improvement during team meetings, praising their enhanced objection handling skills and highlighting specific instances where they successfully overcame objections and closed deals.

By implementing these strategies, sales managers can effectively handle underperforming salespeople, support their growth, and help them improve their sales performance. It demonstrates a commitment to their development, boosts morale, and fosters a culture of continuous improvement within the sales team.

Coaching for Growth and Career Development

Coaching for growth and career development is an essential aspect of sales management. By identifying potential and talent within the sales team, creating individual development plans, and providing coaching for long-term success, sales managers can foster the growth and advancement of their salespeople. This chapter explores the strategies and techniques to effectively coach for growth and career development.

Identifying Potential and Talent

- ✓ Talent Assessment: Conduct a comprehensive talent assessment to identify salespeople with the potential for growth and advancement. Evaluate their performance, skills, and capabilities, as well as their alignment with the organization's future needs. Example: Through performance reviews and observation, a sales manager identifies a salesperson who consistently exceeds targets, demonstrates strong leadership qualities, and exhibits a natural ability to connect with clients. This salesperson shows clear potential for growth and advancement within the organization.
- ✓ Strengths and Areas of Improvement: Understand the strengths and areas of improvement for each salesperson to align their career development plans accordingly. Identify the unique talents and skills that can be leveraged, as well as the areas where further growth is needed.

Example: A sales manager recognizes that a salesperson has exceptional negotiation skills but needs improvement in strategic account management. They tailor the coaching and development plan to focus on enhancing strategic account management abilities while leveraging the salesperson's negotiation strengths.

Creating Individual Development Plans

- ✓ Goal Setting: Collaborate with salespeople to establish meaningful and challenging goals that align with their career aspirations. These goals should be specific, measurable, achievable, relevant, and time-bound (SMART) to provide clarity and focus.

  Example: A salesperson expresses a desire to move into a sales leadership role. The sales manager helps them set SMART goals, such as completing leadership training programs, gaining experience in mentoring junior sales team members, and achieving specific sales targets that demonstrate leadership potential.
- ✓ Skill Development: Identify the skills and competencies required for the salesperson's desired career path. Create a development plan that includes targeted training, workshops, and experiences to enhance these skills.

  Example: A salesperson interested in transitioning into a sales training role needs to develop their presentation and facilitation skills. The sales manager provides opportunities for the salesperson to attend training on effective presentation techniques, assigns them to lead team meetings, and offers feedback and coaching to improve their delivery.

Coaching for Long-Term Success

- ✓ Ongoing Feedback and Support: Provide continuous feedback and support to salespeople throughout their career development journey. Regular coaching conversations help them stay on track, address challenges, and celebrate achievements.

  Example: The sales manager conducts monthly check-ins with salespeople to review progress, discuss challenges, and provide guidance. They offer constructive feedback on performance, recognize milestones achieved, and offer support to overcome obstacles.
- ✓ Stretch Assignments and Opportunities: Offer stretch assignments and growth opportunities that challenge salespeople to expand their skills and knowledge. This helps them gain valuable experience and demonstrates the organization's commitment to their long-term success.

  Example: A salesperson interested in international sales is given the opportunity to lead a cross-border sales initiative. This assignment exposes them to new markets, cultural challenges, and global sales strategies, providing them with valuable experience and fostering their growth.

Coaching for growth and career development is a key responsibility of sales managers. By identifying potential and talent, creating individual development plans, and providing coaching for long-term success, sales managers can support the growth and advancement of their salespeople. This not only benefits the individuals but also contributes to the overall success of the sales team and the organization as a whole.

Coaching for Sales Team Collaboration

Coaching for sales team collaboration is vital for building a cohesive and high-performing sales team. In this chapter, we will explore strategies and techniques for fostering a collaborative culture, conducting team-building exercises and activities, and effectively resolving conflicts within the sales team.

Fostering a Collaborative Culture

- ✓ Clear Communication and Shared Goals: Establish clear lines of communication and ensure that team members understand the shared goals and objectives. Encourage open dialogue, active listening, and the exchange of ideas to foster collaboration.

  Example: The sales manager conducts regular team meetings where each member shares updates, challenges, and best practices. This open communication environment promotes collaboration as team members learn from each other and work together to achieve common goals.
- ✓ Promoting Trust and Psychological Safety: Create an environment of trust and psychological safety where team members feel comfortable sharing their thoughts, opinions, and concerns without fear of judgment or negative consequences. Encourage mutual respect and support among team members.

  Example: The sales manager implements a "no-blame" policy, emphasizing that mistakes are learning opportunities and encouraging team members to take risks and share their experiences. This approach builds trust and psychological safety, leading to increased collaboration and innovation.

Team-Building Exercises and Activities

- ✓ Collaborative Projects: Assign team members to collaborate on projects that require joint effort, problem-solving, and shared responsibility. These projects encourage teamwork, communication, and the development of mutual trust and respect.

  Example: The sales manager assigns a group of salespeople to work on a cross-selling initiative, where they need to collaborate to identify potential cross-selling opportunities, create joint marketing materials, and share leads. This project fosters collaboration and strengthens relationships among team members.
- ✓ Team-Building Workshops: Conduct team-building workshops and activities that focus on enhancing communication, trust, and collaboration within the sales team. These workshops can include problem-solving exercises, role-playing scenarios, and group discussions.

  Example: The sales manager organizes a team-building workshop where team members engage in a collaborative problem-solving activity. They work together to solve a complex sales scenario, leveraging each other's expertise and perspectives to find the best solution. This activity enhances teamwork and collaboration.

Conflict Resolution and Mediation

- ✓ Constructive Conflict Management: Teach sales team members how to manage conflicts in a constructive manner, emphasizing open communication, active listening, and finding mutually beneficial solutions. Provide coaching and guidance on conflict resolution techniques.
  Example: The sales manager conducts a conflict resolution training session for the sales team, teaching them effective communication strategies, active listening techniques, and negotiation skills. Salespeople learn how to address conflicts respectfully and find win-win solutions.
- ✓ Mediation and Facilitation: When conflicts arise within the sales team, the sales manager acts as a mediator or facilitator to help parties understand each other's perspectives, find common ground, and reach a resolution. Provide guidance and support throughout the mediation process.
  Example: The sales manager facilitates a conversation between two sales team members who have conflicting approaches to a particular sales strategy. They create a safe space for both individuals to express their concerns and viewpoints, guiding the discussion towards finding a compromise that combines the best aspects of both approaches.

Coaching for sales team collaboration is crucial for building a cohesive and high-performing sales team. By fostering a collaborative culture, organizing team-building exercises and activities, and effectively resolving conflicts, sales managers can create an environment where teamwork, communication, and collaboration thrive. This leads to increased productivity, innovation, and overall success for the sales team and the organization as a whole.

Measuring Coaching Effectiveness

Measuring the effectiveness of coaching programs is essential to ensure that coaching efforts are yielding desired outcomes and driving improvement in sales performance. In this chapter, we will explore strategies and techniques for evaluating coaching programs, monitoring progress and performance, and continuously improving coaching initiatives.

Evaluating Coaching Programs

- ✓ Goal Achievement: Assess whether coaching programs are effectively contributing to the achievement of predetermined goals and objectives. Measure the extent to which coaching has helped salespeople improve their skills, meet targets, and drive overall sales performance.
  Example: A coaching program aimed at improving negotiation skills can be evaluated by tracking the percentage of successful negotiations and comparing it to pre-coaching benchmarks. If the success rate increases, it indicates that the coaching program has been effective.
- ✓ Participant Feedback: Gather feedback from sales team members who have participated in coaching programs. Use surveys or interviews to understand their perceptions of the coaching experience, its impact on their skills and performance, and their overall satisfaction with the coaching program.
  Example: Distribute a post-coaching program survey asking participants to rate the relevance and usefulness of the coaching

content, their satisfaction with the coach's support, and their perception of the program's impact on their sales performance. Analyze the feedback to identify areas of improvement.

Monitoring Progress and Performance

- ✓ Performance Metrics: Continuously monitor sales performance metrics to assess the impact of coaching on individual and team results. Track key performance indicators (KPIs), such as revenue generated, conversion rates, customer satisfaction scores, and quota attainment, to gauge the effectiveness of coaching efforts.

  Example: Compare the performance metrics of sales team members who have received coaching to those who haven't. If coached individuals consistently outperform their non-coached counterparts, it suggests that coaching has positively influenced their performance.
- ✓ Observations and Assessments: Regularly observe sales team members' interactions, sales calls, and presentations to assess their application of coaching techniques and strategies. Use structured assessment tools to evaluate their competency and progress over time.

  Example: Conduct periodic observations of sales team members' sales calls and assess their adherence to coaching guidance, such as effective questioning techniques, active listening, or objection handling. Compare their performance to coaching benchmarks and provide feedback for improvement.

Continuous Improvement in Coaching

- ✓ Coach Feedback: Encourage sales team members to provide feedback on their coaching experiences. Solicit their suggestions for improvement, additional coaching needs, and any challenges they may have faced during the coaching process.
  Example: Set up regular feedback sessions where sales team members can share their thoughts on the coaching program. This can be done through one-on-one meetings, suggestion boxes, or anonymous surveys. Use the feedback to refine and enhance the coaching program.
- ✓ Review and Adaptation: Continuously review the coaching program's effectiveness and make necessary adjustments based on feedback, evaluation results, and changing business needs. Stay updated on industry trends and best practices to incorporate new coaching techniques and tools.
  Example: Conduct a quarterly review of the coaching program, analyzing the evaluation results, participant feedback, and performance data. Identify areas of improvement and adapt the coaching program accordingly. This may involve updating coaching materials, introducing new training modules, or refining coaching methodologies.

Measuring coaching effectiveness is crucial for evaluating the impact of coaching programs, monitoring sales performance, and driving continuous improvement. By evaluating coaching programs, monitoring progress and performance, and embracing a culture of continuous improvement, sales managers can ensure that coaching initiatives are aligned with organizational goals and consistently deliver positive outcomes. This iterative process fosters ongoing growth and development within the sales team and leads to improved sales performance and overall success.

Gauging the Effectiveness of Coaching Through Various Indicators and Key Performance Metrics

Sales managers can gauge the effectiveness of coaching through various indicators and key performance metrics. Effective coaching should lead to improved sales team performance, increased revenue, and enhanced customer satisfaction. Here are some areas and indicators that can help a sales manager assess the effectiveness of coaching:

1. Sales Performance Metrics:
   - ✓ Sales Revenue: An increase in sales revenue is a clear indicator of effective coaching. A more effective sales team should generate higher revenue.
   - ✓ Conversion Rates: Improved conversion rates, such as lead-to-opportunity or opportunity-to-close ratios, indicate that coaching is effective in helping salespeople close deals.
   - ✓ Sales Cycle Length: A reduction in the length of the sales cycle can indicate that salespeople are more adept at moving prospects through the buying process.
2. Individual and Team Quota Attainment:
   - ✓ Check if more team members consistently meet or exceed their sales quotas after coaching.
3. Lead and Prospect Management:
   - ✓ Assess whether leads are being effectively managed, leading to a higher volume of qualified leads and prospects.

- ✓ Review whether salespeople are effectively nurturing leads through the sales funnel, from initial contact to closing the deal.

4. Customer Satisfaction and Retention:
   - ✓ A rise in customer satisfaction and retention rates can indicate that the sales team is better at understanding and meeting customer needs.
5. Pipeline Growth:
   - ✓ An increase in the size and health of the sales pipeline is an indicator of effective coaching, as it suggests more opportunities for future revenue.
6. Win Rates:
   - ✓ Improved win rates demonstrate that salespeople are becoming more skilled at securing deals.
7. Response to Objections:
   - ✓ Monitor how effectively salespeople respond to objections and concerns raised by prospects. A higher rate of objection handling success can indicate effective coaching.
8. Sales KPIs:
   - ✓ Review key performance indicators (KPIs) such as average deal size, customer acquisition cost, and lifetime value to evaluate whether these metrics are improving.
9. Knowledge and Skill Improvement:
   - ✓ Gauge the sales team's knowledge and skills development by evaluating their ability to articulate product features, benefits, and competitive advantages.
10. Feedback from Sales Team:

- ✓ Collect feedback from sales team members on the impact of coaching. Are they finding it beneficial and relevant?

11. Observation and Role-Playing:

- ✓ Observe sales team interactions with customers and prospects. Are they implementing the techniques and strategies discussed in coaching sessions effectively?
- ✓ Role-playing exercises can help assess how well salespeople are putting coaching into practice.

12. Coaching Plan Progress:

- ✓ Review the progress and achievement of goals set during coaching sessions. Are salespeople meeting their action plans?

13. Sales Team Morale and Engagement:

- ✓ High morale, job satisfaction, and engagement can indicate that coaching is contributing to a positive work environment.

14. Customer Feedback:

- ✓ Gather feedback from customers about their interactions with the sales team. Positive customer feedback often correlates with effective coaching.

15. Continuous Improvement:

- ✓ Evaluate whether sales team members are actively seeking feedback, self-reflecting, and demonstrating a commitment to continuous improvement.

16. Competitive Advantage:

- ✓ Assess if the sales team's ability to communicate the unique value of products or services gives the organization a competitive advantage.

17. Post-Sale Service and Support:

- ✓ Measure post-sale service quality and support, as effective coaching should lead to improved customer service.

18. Referrals and Up-selling:

- ✓ A higher rate of referrals and successful up-selling can indicate that the sales team is skilled at building long-term relationships.

Assessing these areas and indicators will help sales managers determine the effectiveness of coaching initiatives and make data-driven decisions to further enhance the sales team's performance and success.

Coaching for Sales Managers

Coaching is not only essential for the development of sales team members but also for the growth and effectiveness of sales managers themselves. In this chapter, we will explore the importance of self-coaching for sales managers, the benefits of peer coaching and mentoring, and the significance of coaching support for sales managers.

Self-Coaching for Sales Managers

- ✓ Reflective Practice: Encourage sales managers to engage in reflective practice, where they critically analyze their own performance, decisions, and behaviors. This self-reflection enables managers to identify areas for improvement and develop action plans to enhance their coaching effectiveness. Example: After a challenging sales meeting, a sales manager takes time to reflect on their communication style, level of engagement, and the effectiveness of their coaching interventions. They identify areas where they could have provided clearer guidance and plan to adjust their approach for future coaching sessions.
- ✓ Goal Setting and Accountability: Sales managers should set personal development goals and hold themselves accountable for achieving them. By setting specific objectives and regularly assessing their progress, managers can enhance their coaching skills and overcome any personal limitations or blind spots.

Example: A sales manager sets a goal to improve their active listening skills during coaching sessions. They implement strategies such as summarizing and paraphrasing to ensure they fully understand the concerns and perspectives of their team members. They monitor their progress through self-assessment and seek feedback from their team.

Peer Coaching and Mentoring

- ✓ Peer Coaching: Encourage sales managers to engage in peer coaching relationships with other managers within the organization. Peer coaching provides a valuable opportunity for managers to share experiences, exchange insights, and provide support and feedback to each other.

  Example: Two sales managers form a peer coaching partnership, where they regularly meet to discuss challenges, share best practices, and provide constructive feedback. They observe each other's coaching sessions, offer suggestions for improvement, and celebrate each other's successes.
- ✓ Mentoring Relationships: Encourage sales managers to seek out mentorship from more experienced managers or leaders within the organization. Mentors can provide guidance, share their expertise, and offer valuable insights to help managers enhance their coaching skills and professional development.

  Example: A sales manager identifies a seasoned sales leader as their mentor. They schedule regular mentoring sessions to discuss coaching strategies, career development, and personal growth. The mentor shares real-life experiences and provides guidance on handling complex coaching scenarios.

Coaching Support for Sales Managers

- ✓ Training and Development: Provide sales managers with ongoing training and development opportunities to enhance their coaching skills. Offer workshops, seminars, or online courses specifically tailored for sales managers to deepen their coaching knowledge and refine their techniques.

  Example: The organization conducts a coaching skills training program exclusively for sales managers. The training covers advanced coaching methodologies, effective feedback techniques, and strategies for coaching in challenging situations. Sales managers participate in interactive exercises and receive personalized coaching feedback.
- ✓ Coaching Resources and Tools: Equip sales managers with resources and tools that support their coaching efforts. These can include coaching templates, assessment tools, coaching frameworks, and access to industry research and best practices.

  Example: The organization provides sales managers with a coaching toolkit that includes a variety of resources, such as a performance evaluation template, a goal-setting worksheet, and a library of coaching articles and videos. These resources help managers structure their coaching sessions and stay updated on coaching trends.

Coaching for sales managers is essential for their own growth, development, and effectiveness as leaders. By practicing self-coaching, engaging in peer coaching and mentoring relationships, and receiving coaching support, sales managers can enhance their coaching skills, overcome challenges, and foster a culture of continuous improvement within their teams. This commitment to their own development enables sales managers to provide impactful coaching that drives sales team success and contributes to the overall achievement of organizational goals.

Leading with Coaching

Leaders who incorporate coaching into their leadership style can significantly impact their teams' performance and drive organizational success. In this chapter, we will explore the integration of coaching into leadership, the importance of inspiring and influencing others, and how coaching contributes to overall organizational success.

Integrating Coaching into Leadership

- ✓ Coaching Mindset: Effective leaders embrace a coaching mindset by viewing their role as that of a coach rather than a traditional manager. They prioritize the growth and development of their team members and empower them to reach their full potential.

  Example: A sales leader adopts a coaching mindset by actively seeking opportunities to support and guide their team members. Instead of providing all the answers, they encourage their team to find their own solutions by asking powerful questions and fostering independent thinking.
- ✓ Coaching Conversations: Leaders integrate coaching into their day-to-day interactions by engaging in coaching conversations with their team members. These conversations focus on individual development, goal setting, and problem-solving.

  Example: During a coaching conversation, a leader helps a team member identify their strengths and areas for improvement. They collaboratively set specific goals and create action plans to address skill gaps. The leader provides ongoing support and feedback to ensure progress and growth.

Inspiring and Influencing Others

- ✓ Vision and Purpose: Leaders inspire their teams by sharing a compelling vision and connecting it to each team member's purpose. They communicate the bigger picture, instill a sense of purpose, and align individual goals with the organization's objectives.

  Example: A sales leader communicates a vision of becoming the industry leader known for exceptional customer service. They inspire their team by emphasizing the positive impact their work has on customers' lives, motivating them to deliver outstanding results.
- ✓ Building Relationships: Effective leaders build strong relationships with their team members based on trust, respect, and empathy. They invest time in getting to know their team members on a personal level and understanding their aspirations and challenges.

  Example: A leader takes the time to have regular one-on-one meetings with each team member, actively listening to their concerns, providing guidance, and offering support. By showing genuine care and interest, the leader fosters a trusting and collaborative relationship.

Coaching for Organizational Success

- ✓ Talent Development: Leaders who coach prioritize the development of their team members' skills and competencies. They identify high-potential individuals, nurture their talents, and provide opportunities for growth and advancement.

Example: A sales leader identifies a team member with exceptional leadership potential. They assign the team member to lead a strategic project, provide guidance and support throughout the process, and offer coaching to enhance their leadership skills.

- ✓ Performance Culture: Leaders who integrate coaching into their leadership style contribute to creating a performance-focused culture. They set clear expectations, provide constructive feedback, and recognize and reward achievements.

  Example: A leader establishes a culture of continuous improvement by regularly reviewing performance, providing timely feedback, and recognizing outstanding achievements. They encourage team members to set challenging goals, celebrate progress, and provide coaching support to reach new levels of performance.

Leading with coaching involves integrating coaching principles into leadership, inspiring and influencing team members, and leveraging coaching for organizational success. By adopting a coaching mindset, engaging in coaching conversations, inspiring through vision and purpose, building strong relationships, and prioritizing talent development, leaders can create an environment where individuals thrive and contribute to the overall success of the organization. Coaching-centered leadership fosters employee engagement, boosts performance, and drives sustainable growth.

Do’s and Don’ts of Coaching for a Sales Manager

Here's a list of 20 Do's and 20 Don'ts of coaching for a sales manager:

Do's of Coaching:

1. Set Clear Objectives: Clearly define the objectives and expected outcomes of coaching sessions.
2. Active Listening: Practice active listening to understand the salesperson's perspective and challenges.
3. Provide Constructive Feedback: Offer specific, actionable feedback that helps the salesperson improve.
4. Individualize Coaching: Tailor coaching to each salesperson's unique needs and strengths.
5. Recognize Achievements: Acknowledge and celebrate both small and significant achievements.
6. Promote Self-Reflection: Encourage salespeople to reflect on their performance and identify areas for improvement.
7. Foster a Growth Mindset: Cultivate a culture where learning and growth are valued and supported.
8. Role-Playing: Use role-playing exercises to practice and improve sales techniques.
9. Follow Up: Ensure that the action plans and goals set during coaching sessions are followed up on.

10. Leverage Technology: Use sales and CRM tools to gather data and provide data-driven coaching.
11. Create Safe Spaces: Foster an environment where salespeople feel safe sharing concerns and seeking help.
12. Empower Problem Solving: Encourage salespeople to come up with their solutions to challenges.
13. Regular Check-Ins: Maintain regular communication and check-ins with salespeople to monitor progress.
14. Offer Skill Development: Provide access to training and resources for skill improvement.
15. Focus on Strengths: Recognize and build on the salesperson's strengths while addressing weaknesses.
16. Be Supportive: Offer emotional support, especially during challenging times.
17. Goal Setting: Collaboratively set achievable and motivating goals for the salesperson.
18. Exemplify Coaching: Lead by example by embodying the coaching principles you preach.
19. Continuous Improvement: Continuously improve your coaching techniques based on feedback and results.
20. Measure Impact: Assess and measure the impact of coaching on performance and adjust strategies accordingly.

Don'ts of Coaching:

1. Don't Be Overcritical: Avoid being overly critical or negative in your feedback.

2. Don't Micromanage: Avoid micromanaging salespeople during coaching sessions or in general.
3. Don't Be Disengaged: Don't be disengaged or uninterested during coaching sessions.
4. Don't Ignore Personal Development: Don't solely focus on metrics and neglect personal and professional development.
5. Don't Compare: Avoid comparing salespeople against each other; focus on individual growth.
6. Don't Rush: Don't rush through coaching sessions; take the time to address concerns thoroughly.
7. Don't Disregard Emotional Intelligence: Don't disregard the emotional aspect of coaching; be empathetic.
8. Don't Be Inflexible: Avoid rigid coaching approaches; be adaptable to different personalities and learning styles.
9. Don't Overload: Don't overwhelm salespeople with too much information or advice in one session.
10. Don't Neglect Feedback: Don't withhold feedback or let issues fester without addressing them.
11. Don't Dictate Solutions: Avoid dictating solutions; let salespeople participate in problem-solving.
12. Don't Ignore Feedback: Don't ignore or dismiss feedback from salespeople regarding coaching effectiveness.
13. Don't Neglect Celebrations: Don't forget to celebrate successes and milestones achieved during coaching.

14. Don't Be Inconsistent: Avoid inconsistency in your coaching approach; be reliable and predictable.
15. Don't Neglect Training: Don't neglect ongoing training and development; coaching should be a continuous process.
16. Don't Isolate Coaching: Don't isolate coaching from the overall sales strategy and goals of the organization.
17. Don't Ignore Ethics: Don't compromise ethical standards in pursuit of sales goals.
18. Don't Be One-Dimensional: Don't focus solely on sales techniques; consider the holistic growth of the salesperson.
19. Don't Make Assumptions: Don't assume you know the underlying issues without consulting the salesperson.
20. Don't Discontinue Coaching: Don't stop coaching once a certain level of performance is achieved; maintain the coaching process to sustain growth.

These Do's and Don'ts provide guidance on how to effectively coach sales teams while avoiding common pitfalls and fostering a culture of continuous improvement and success.

Coaching Templates and Checklists-Examples

Given below is a collection of customizable templates and checklists that can be used in various coaching scenarios. These tools are designed to help sales managers structure and enhance their coaching efforts.

Template 1: Coaching Session Plan

Use this template to plan your coaching sessions effectively. It provides a structured outline for your coaching conversation.

Coaching Session Plan

- Date: [Insert Date]
- Coachee's Name: [Insert Coachee's Name]
- Coach's Name: [Insert Coach's Name]
- Goal for This Session: [Insert Coaching Session Goal]

Agenda

1. Opening:
☐ Build Rapport
☐ Set Expectations
2. Current Situation (Reality):
☐ Discuss Current Performance
☐ Identify Challenges
3. Goal Setting (Goal):
☐ Define Specific Goals
☐ Set Objectives
4. Options and Strategies:
☐ Brainstorm Solutions
☐ Discuss Action Plans

5. Commitment and Follow-Up:
□ Agree on Next Steps
□ Set Timeline
6. Closing and Feedback:
□ Summarize Key Points
□ Receive Feedback

Template 2: Coaching Feedback Form

This form allows you to gather feedback from your coachees after coaching sessions to continuously improve your coaching skills.

Coaching Feedback Form

- Date: [Insert Date]
- Coachee's Name: [Insert Coachee's Name]
- Coach's Name: [Insert Coach's Name]

1. Session Evaluation

- Rate the coaching session on a scale of 1 to 5, with 5 being excellent.
- Overall Session Rating: [Rating]

2. Communication

How would you rate the coach's communication skills?
□ Excellent
□ Good
□ Satisfactory
□ Needs Improvement

3. Goal Clarity

Were the coaching session goals clear to you?
□ Yes
□ No
If no, please provide details: [Insert Comments]

4. Progress

Did you make progress toward your goals during this session?

☐ Yes

☐ No

If no, please explain: [Insert Comments]

5. Suggestions for Improvement

- What suggestions do you have for the coach to enhance future coaching sessions? [Insert Comments]

6. Additional Comments

- Please share any additional comments or thoughts regarding the coaching session. [Insert Comments]

Template 3: Sales Performance Evaluation Checklist

This checklist is used to assess a salesperson's overall performance and identify areas for improvement.

Sales Performance Evaluation Checklist

- Salesperson's Name: [Insert Salesperson's Name]
- Date of Evaluation: [Insert Date]

1. Sales Skills and Techniques

☐ Effective Communication

☐ Active Listening

☐ Handling Objections

☐ Closing Sales

☐ Relationship Building

2. Goal Achievement

☐ Meeting Sales Targets

☐ Achieving Objectives

☐ Sales Growth

☐ Customer Retention

3. Product Knowledge

☐ In-Depth Product Knowledge
☐ Ability to Explain Product Benefits
☐ Handling Product-Related Questions/ Concerns

4. Time Management

☐ Effective Time Management
☐ Prioritizing Sales Activities
☐ Meeting Deadlines

5. Professionalism

☐ Presentation and Attire
☐ Customer Service
☐ Attitude & Behavior
☐ Habits
☐ Ethical Sales Practices

6. Self-Development

☐ Participation in Training
☐ Seeking Feedback
☐ Skill Enhancement

7. Comments and Recommendations

- Provide specific comments on the salesperson's performance and any recommendations for improvement. [Insert Comments]

These templates and checklists can be customized and incorporated into your coaching process to ensure a structured and effective approach. Use them as a foundation and adapt them to suit your specific coaching needs and preferences.

Future Trends in Sales Coaching

As the business landscape continues to evolve, so does the field of sales coaching. In this chapter, we will explore the emerging trends in sales coaching, including the integration of AI and automation, the rise of virtual coaching in remote teams, and the evolving role of sales managers as coaches.

AI and Automation in Sales Coaching

- ✓ AI-Driven Insights: AI technologies can provide valuable insights and data-driven recommendations to sales coaches. These tools can analyze large volumes of data, identify patterns, and offer personalized coaching recommendations based on individual performance and customer behavior.

  Example: AI-powered sales coaching platforms can analyze sales call recordings to detect key moments of successful persuasion and provide feedback on specific techniques or strategies that led to positive outcomes.
- ✓ Automated Coaching Support: Automation tools can assist sales coaches by automating certain coaching processes, such as scheduling coaching sessions, sending reminders, and tracking progress. This automation frees up coaches' time, allowing them to focus on more strategic aspects of coaching.

  Example: A sales coaching platform with automated features can send regular performance reports to sales team members, highlighting their progress, areas for improvement, and recommended resources for skill development.

Virtual Coaching and Remote Teams

- ✓ Virtual Coaching Platforms: With the rise of remote work and distributed teams, virtual coaching platforms enable sales coaches to deliver coaching sessions and support remotely. These platforms provide features for video conferencing, screen sharing, and document collaboration.
  Example: A sales coach conducts virtual coaching sessions using a video conferencing platform, where they can share sales presentations, review performance dashboards, and provide real-time feedback to team members located in different geographical locations.
- ✓ Asynchronous Coaching: Virtual coaching also allows for asynchronous coaching, where coaches and team members can engage in coaching interactions at their convenience. This flexibility accommodates different time zones and work schedules.
  Example: A sales coach records a coaching video with specific feedback and sends it to a sales representative who can watch it at their convenience. The representative can then respond with questions or comments, initiating an ongoing coaching dialogue.

Evolving Role of Sales Managers as Coaches

- ✓ Strategic Coaching Partners: Sales managers are increasingly seen as strategic coaching partners who guide their teams towards achieving organizational goals. They provide guidance on long-term career development,

align individual objectives with business objectives, and support skill acquisition.
Example: A sales manager partners with a sales representative to identify growth opportunities, create a personalized development plan, and regularly review progress towards career advancement within the organization.

- ✓ Performance Coaches: Sales managers play a critical role in driving performance excellence within their teams. They provide ongoing feedback, facilitate skill-building workshops, and implement performance improvement strategies.
Example: A sales manager conducts a performance coaching session with a team member to address specific skill gaps. They provide targeted resources, arrange training sessions, and assign practice exercises to help the team member improve their performance.

The future of sales coaching is shaped by the integration of AI and automation, the rise of virtual coaching in remote teams, and the evolving role of sales managers as strategic partners and performance coaches. By embracing these trends, organizations can enhance coaching effectiveness, reach geographically dispersed teams, and leverage data-driven insights to drive sales performance and achieve long-term success in a dynamic business landscape. Sales coaches and managers who adapt to these emerging trends will be well-positioned to maximize the potential of their teams and stay ahead of the competition.

Taking it Forward

Congratulations on completing the journey through **'Coaching Skills for Sales Managers -** *Making the Great Stride from Manager to an Effective Coach.'* Throughout this book, we have explored the fundamental principles, techniques, and strategies required to transition from being a manager to becoming an effective coach for your sales team.

In this concluding chapter, let us reflect on the key concepts covered, summarize the important takeaways, and offer final thoughts and action steps to empower you as a sales manager and coach.

Recap of Key Concepts:

- ✓ The Coaching Mindset: We emphasized the importance of adopting a coaching mindset, which involves shifting your focus from simply managing tasks and results to developing the skills, potential, and success of your sales team members.
- ✓ Building Relationships: We discussed the significance of establishing trust, practicing effective communication, and active listening in building strong and meaningful relationships with your team. These elements form the foundation for successful coaching interactions.
- ✓ Setting Clear Expectations: We explored the process of defining goals and objectives, using SMART goals in sales coaching, and aligning individual goals with organizational goals. Clear expectations help create clarity, focus, and accountability within your sales team.

- ✓ Assessing Performance: We delved into performance metrics, key performance indicators (KPIs), and various techniques for evaluating performance. Providing constructive feedback enables your team members to grow and improve their sales effectiveness.
- ✓ Coaching Techniques and Tools: We explored different coaching approaches, coaching models and frameworks like GROW and OSKAR, and the effective use of technology in coaching. These techniques and tools provide structure and guidance for your coaching sessions.
- ✓ Developing Sales Skills: We emphasized the importance of identifying skill gaps, tailoring coaching to individual needs, and coaching for sales techniques and strategies. Developing the skills of your team members enhances their performance and contributes to overall sales success.
- ✓ Motivating and Inspiring Sales Teams: We discussed understanding motivation factors, building a motivating environment, and utilizing incentives and recognition to inspire your sales team. Motivated individuals are more likely to achieve their goals and exceed expectations.
- ✓ Overcoming Challenges in Sales Coaching: We explored strategies for addressing resistance to coaching, dealing with difficult conversations, and handling underperforming salespeople. Overcoming these challenges requires effective communication, empathy, and problem-solving skills.

- ✓ Coaching for Growth and Career Development: We highlighted the importance of identifying potential and talent, creating individual development plans, and coaching for long-term success. Helping your team members grow and develop their careers strengthens their commitment and loyalty.
- ✓ Coaching for Sales Team Collaboration: We discussed fostering a collaborative culture, team-building exercises and activities, and conflict resolution and mediation. Collaboration enhances teamwork, communication, and synergy within your sales team.
- ✓ Measuring Coaching Effectiveness: We explored techniques for evaluating coaching programs, monitoring progress and performance, and continuous improvement in coaching. Measuring effectiveness helps you refine your coaching approach and ensure its impact on sales outcomes.
- ✓ Coaching for Sales Managers: We emphasized the value of self-coaching for sales managers, peer coaching and mentoring, and coaching support for sales managers. Continuous self-improvement and collaboration with other managers contribute to your effectiveness as a coach.
- ✓ Leading with Coaching: We discussed integrating coaching into leadership, inspiring and influencing others, and coaching for organizational success. Leading with a coaching approach creates a positive and high-performance culture within your sales team.

Final Thoughts and Action Steps:

Now that you have acquired a comprehensive understanding of coaching skills for sales managers, it is essential to translate this knowledge into action. Here are some final thoughts and action steps to guide you on your journey:

- ✓ Embrace the Coaching Mindset: Continuously remind yourself of the coaching principles and the impact they can have on your sales team. Approach each interaction as an opportunity to coach and develop your team members.
- ✓ Practice, Practice, Practice: Put your coaching skills into action by engaging in regular coaching conversations with your team. Apply the coaching techniques and models discussed in this book and adapt them to suit the unique needs of your team members.
- ✓ Seek Feedback and Learn: Actively seek feedback from your team members and colleagues to gauge the effectiveness of your coaching efforts. Embrace a growth mindset and continuously learn and improve your coaching skills based on feedback and self-reflection.
- ✓ Invest in Development: Commit to ongoing learning and development in the field of coaching. Attend workshops, seminars, and conferences, and explore resources that can enhance your coaching abilities and keep you up to date with the latest trends and practices.
- ✓ Celebrate Successes: Recognize and celebrate the successes and achievements of your team members. Use incentives, rewards, and recognition programs to acknowledge

their efforts and foster a positive and motivating environment.

- ✓ Emphasize Collaboration: Foster a collaborative culture within your sales team by encouraging teamwork, facilitating open communication, and providing opportunities for collaboration. Leverage team-building exercises and activities to strengthen relationships and enhance team dynamics.
- ✓ Measure and Adapt: Regularly evaluate the impact of your coaching efforts. Monitor performance metrics, solicit feedback, and make adjustments as needed. Embrace a continuous improvement mindset and seek opportunities to refine and enhance your coaching approach.

By mastering the art of coaching, you are making a significant leap from being a manager to becoming a leader who inspires, develops, and empowers their sales team. Remember, coaching is an ongoing journey of growth and learning. It requires dedication, practice, and a genuine commitment to the success of your team members.

Through the application of the coaching skills, techniques, and strategies outlined in this book, you have the power to transform not only your own leadership style but also the performance and success of your sales team. Embrace the coaching mindset, build strong relationships, set clear expectations, assess performance, and continuously strive for growth and improvement.

Thank you for embarking on this journey of becoming a skilled sales manager and coach. Your dedication to honing your coaching skills will undoubtedly lead to enhanced sales performance, increased motivation, and the long-term success of your team. Best of luck on your coaching endeavors!

About the Author 'GERARD ASSEY'

Gerard Assey is a Graduate in Economics, a PGD in Management (HRD) and holds a Doctorate in Leadership. Gerard holds several International Qualifications in Sales, Debt Collection, Training & Teaching, and is a 'Fellow' of the prestigious 'Institute of Sales & Marketing Management'-UK, a Certified NLP Practitioner, a 'Certified Trainer', an 'Accredited Management Teacher-Behavioral Sciences', a 'Certified Competency Facilitator', a 'Certified Management Consultant'- (the International credentials of a professional management consultant, awarded in accordance with global standards of the ICMCI); and a Certification from the University of Michigan in 'Successful Negotiation: Essential Strategies and Skills'

He is also a Member of the 'National Association of Sales Professionals' backed with several years experience in varied industries, both in India and Overseas. He also holds an 'Etiquette Consultant' Certification from the USA (by Sue Fox, Author of Best Seller: 'Business Etiquette for Dummies'. She has trained some of the top celebrities' world over). He was also a recipient of a scholarship for extensive training in Japan on 'Corporate Management for India'.

Gerard Assey is 'Founder & Chief Corporate Trainer' of the Group: '**Citius, Altius, Fortius Unlimited**'- an organization that **celebrated 20 years of Glorious Service** in 2021, focusing on 3 Core Competencies:

People. Performance. Profit; in functional areas of Sales & Marketing, HR & Organizational Development, covering Recruitment, Training & Consultancy!

Having managed organizations with large Sales Forces in India & Overseas, his specialization cover extensive areas of Sales Training (All levels - Presentation, Negotiation, Key/ Strategic Accounts Management & Managerial Skills for all sectors), Bid Proposal/ Capture Planning/ Management Trainings, Retail Sales, Customer Service & Customer Retention Programs, Training for Prevention & Collection of Debt, Self & Personal Development Programs (Time Management, Teamwork & Team Building, Business Etiquette & Personal Grooming, Leadership & Managerial Skills, People Management Skills, Train-the-Trainer etc), including preparation of Custom-designed Business Manuals for Internal (HR, Induction, and Sales etc) & External use (Instruction, User Manuals).

Gerard has successfully conducted over 6000 Trainings & Workshops (as of Oct '23) all across India, Middle East, Africa, Europe & S.E. Asia. Besides public programs conducted regularly, both in India & Overseas, he has some of the top names as clients whom he services from Single Owners to large Public & Government undertakings, covering all sectors, for their in-house needs.

His website: www.CollectionSkills.com is the only one in this part of the world to be featured in the 'Collections & Credit Risk Magazine-USA' under 'Who's Who in Training' and ranks TOP, along with other websites listed below on most search engines.

Gerard is author of 88 books already (Nov 2023),

A few of our business related books:

1. Bite-sized Bits on Commonsense Management
2. Heart to Heart on Life's Principles'
3. How to become a Successful Manager
4. The Sales Professionals' Master Workbook of S.Y.S.T.E.M.S
5. The Professional Business Email Etiquette Handbook & Guide
6. The Professional Business Video-Conferencing Etiquette Handbook & Guide
7. Professional Presentation Skills
8. Exceptional Customer Service
9. Professional Tele-Marketing Skills
10. Professional Debt Collection Skills
11. The G.R.E.A.T. Sales & Service Workbook
12. Sales Training Advantage for Results (*The Ultimate Sales Training Manual to enable you stand out as a S.T.A.R.*)
13. CEO Daily Planner & Organizer
14. The Sales Professionals' Master Daily Planner
15. The Professional Debt Collector's Master Daily Planner
16. My Daily Planner & Organizer
17. MY EMERGENCY INFORMATION RECORD (Family Emergency & Peace of Mind Planner)
18. The Ultimate Therapist & Counselors Planner and Organizer
19. Building an Ethical Workplace
20. Managing Relationships at Work
21. Managing Business Meetings Effectively
22. Effective Delegation Skills
23. Goal Setting for Success
24. B2B Selling by Email
25. Professional Business Etiquette & Grooming
26. Dining Etiquette & Table Manners
27. Effective Networking Skills
28. Grooming, Etiquette & Manners for Teens, Young Adults & Future Leaders
29. Inter-Personal Skills
30. Get Ready, Get Hired!
31. Selling in a Recession
32. Effective Receivables Management in an Economic Downturn!
33. Real Estate & Property Sales Training

34. Credit Sales & Accounts Receivable Management
35. Selling Skills for Real Estate & Property Advisors
36. Take G.R.E.A.T. C.A.R.E!
37. Spa, Salon & Health Club Selling Skills
38. Selling Travel, Holiday & MICE Services
39. Selling Skills for Spa's, Salons & Health Clubs
40. Retailing in Salons & Spas
41. Selling Holiday, Vacation, Tours & Packages
42. The Power of Sales Referrals
43. Selling Luxury
44. Technical Selling Skills
45. Financial Advisors Sales Training
46. Dealing with Burnout at Work Monopolize Your Markets
47. Selling to Affluent Customers
48. Growing up with Grace
49. Financial Selling Skills
50. *The Effective Manager's Guide: Key Skills to Thrive*
51. From Aspiring to Inspiring: A Guide for New Managers on the Rise
52. The Power of Focus
53. Selling with Integrity: Sell Like Jesus The Perfect Role Model!
54. 31 Habits of Champions: Your 31-Day Journey to Greatness
55. Rejecting Grasshopper Talk: From Grasshopper to Giant-Killer-*Defeating Giants Daily!*
56. Navigate the AI-Powered Future of Bid & Proposals: Up-Skill to Stay Relevant with Alternative Career Paths & Opportunities
57. Hiring Sales Winners
58. Present with Impact
59. Success Unlocked: *Breaking Free from Habits that Hold You Back*
60. Complaints to Cheers, Feedback to Gold: Mastering Complaints Management
61. Thriving Together: *Cultivating Diversity, Equity, and Inclusion*
62. Coaching Skills for Sales Managers

Besides regularly contributing to business & trade journals, including international ones such as the 'Creative Training Techniques' and the 'Sales News'

of the U.S.A, He is also a member of several prestigious bodies & trade associations, having participated in many Conferences & Workshops in India & Overseas.
Prior to his last assignment of leading & managing a large MNC as head, Gerard had a 3-year stint in the Middle East as a Consultant with a leading British Consultancy Firm.

As the past 'Official Country Representative' for the International Business Award- 'THE STEVIES'-(the business world's own Oscar) for about 4 years- he ensured a few Indian companies that qualify for the same every year!

Gerard can be contacted at:
Email: training@Sales-Training.in,training@CollectionSkills.com
Websites:

www.Sales-Training.in
www.EtiquetteWorks.in
www.CollectionSkills.com
www.RetailSalesTraining.in
www.SalesTrainingIndia.com
www.ManualPreparation.com
www.TrainingWithPuppets.com
www.FirstContactAcademy.com
www.SalesAndMarketingRecruiter.com

Our TRAININGS that can help your team

- ✓ **Sales Effectiveness**: Selling Skills for any Sector: Service/ Logistics/ FMCG Realty/ Insurance & Finance/ Media/ SPA's, Health Clubs & Salons/ Key Account Management, Effective Negotiation Skills/ Bid & Proposal Management Skills/ Retail Sales Training: Any Sector (Auto, Jewelry, Clothing, Luxury etc)
- ✓ **Customer Service Skills**-Complaints Handling & Customer Retention
- ✓ **Debt Prevention & Collection Skills**
- ✓ **Etiquette & Grooming**
- ✓ **Leadership & Managerial Skills**
- ✓ **Self & Personal Development Skills**: Presentation Skills/ Effective Communication Skills/Business Proposal Writing Skills/ Problem Solving & Decision Making Skills/ Empowering Secretaries-The perfect PA! (For Secretaries & PA's)/ Effective Time Management/ Teamwork & Teambuilding/ P.R.I.D.E- **P**ersonal **R**esponsibility **I**n **D**elivering **E**xcellence

www.ingramcontent.com/pod-product-compliance
Lightning Source LLC
Chambersburg PA
CBHW062108160726
48282CB00026B/708
* 9 7 8 9 3 9 2 4 9 2 2 3 5 *